THE TRUTH ABOUT

the lordship of

Christ

[handwritten inscription:]

a. B. Brown
JUNE 8 - 2013
Rockingham NC

THE TRUTH ABOUT

the lordship of
Christ

John MacArthur

THOMAS NELSON
Since 1798

NASHVILLE   DALLAS   MEXICO CITY   RIO DE JANEIRO

Published in Nashville, Tennessee, by Thomas Nelson. Thomas Nelson is a registered trademark of Thomas Nelson, Inc.

Thomas Nelson, Inc., titles may be purchased in bulk for educational, business, fund-raising, or sales promotional use. For information, please e-mail SpecialMarkets@ThomasNelson.com.

Compiled from previously published material in *The God Who Loves, Truth for Today, The Vanishing Conscience, Hard to Believe, The Gospel According to the Apostles*, and *Welcome to the Family*.

Library of Congress Cataloging-in-Publication Data

MacArthur, John, 1939-
  The truth about the lordship of Christ / John MacArthur.
     p. cm.
  Includes bibliographical references (p.   ).
  ISBN 978-1-4002-0416-8
1. Jesus Christ--Lordship. I. Title.
  BT270.M33 2012
  232'.8--dc23

Printed in the United States of America

12 13 14 15 16 QG 6 5 4 3 2 1

CONTENTS

CHAPTER 1

LORD OF THE UNIVERSE

Christians have many reasons for rejoicing. The primary one is based on who God is—He is sovereign. That is the single greatest truth about God. Nothing is outside His control, and He controls everything to work out ultimately for our good (Romans 8:28). He has an infinite understanding of every aspect of our lives— where we are and what we say (Psalm 139:2–4). And He exercises His understanding in perfect wisdom. Knowing God like that should give us inexpressible and glorious joy.

The believer who doesn't live in the confidence of God's sovereignty will lack His peace and be left to the chaos of a troubled heart. But our confident trust in the Lord will allow us to thank Him in the midst of trials because we have God's peace on duty to protect our hearts and minds.

God can do whatever He wants because He is God, and His decrees carry the full weight of divine sovereignty. God spoke, and the worlds were created. "What is seen was not made out of things which are visible" (Hebrews 11:3 NASB). He spoke things that were not, and behold! They were. He can call people, places, and events into existence solely by His divinely sovereign decrees. He can declare believing sinners righteous even though they are not. That is justification.

JUSTIFICATION AND LORDSHIP

But justification never occurs alone in God's plan. It is always accompanied by sanctification. God does not declare sinners righteous legally without making them righteous practically. Justification is not just a legal fiction. When God declares someone righteous, He will inevitably bring it to pass. "Whom He justified, these He also glorified" (Romans 8:30). When justification occurs, the process of sanctification begins. Grace always encompasses both.

I am convinced from Scripture that God is absolutely sovereign in the salvation of sinners. Salvation "does not depend on the man who wills or the man who runs, but on God who has mercy" (Romans 9:16 NASB). We are redeemed not because of anything good in us, but because God chose us unto salvation. He chose certain individuals and passed over others, and He made that choice in eternity past, before the foundation of the world (Ephesians 1:4). Moreover, He chose without regard to anything He foresaw in the elect; simply "according to the good pleasure of his will [and] to the praise of the glory of his grace" (vv. 5–6 KJV). Election arises from the love of God. Those whom He chose, He "loved . . . with an everlasting love [and drew them to Himself] with lovingkindness" (Jeremiah 31:3).

But certainly we can affirm those truths without also concluding that God's attitude toward the non-elect is one of utter hatred.

LOVE AND HATE

I am troubled by the tendency of some—often young people newly infatuated with Reformed doctrine—who insist that God cannot possibly love those who never repent and believe. I encounter this view, it seems, with increasing frequency. The argument inevitably goes like this: Psalm 7:11 tells us "God is angry with the wicked every day." It seems reasonable to assume that if God loved everyone, He would have chosen everyone unto salvation. Therefore, God does not love the non-elect. Those who hold this view often go to great lengths to argue that John 3:16 cannot really mean God loves the whole world.

Perhaps the best-known argument for this view is found in the unabridged edition of an otherwise excellent book, *The Sovereignty of God*, by A. W. Pink.[1] Pink wrote, "God loves whom He chooses. He does not love everybody."[2] Later in the book, he added this:

Is it true that God loves the one who is despising and rejecting His blessed Son? God is Light as well as Love, and therefore His love must be a holy love. To tell the Christ-rejecter that God loves him is to cauterize his conscience, as well as to afford him a sense of security in his sins. The fact is, that the love of God, is a truth for the saints only, and to present it to the enemies of God is to take the children's bread and cast it to the dogs. With the exception of John 3:16, not once in the four gospels do we read of the Lord Jesus—the perfect teacher—telling sinners that God loved them![3]

In an appendix to the unabridged edition, Pink argued that the word *world* in John 3:16 ("For God so loved the *world* . . .") "refers to *the world of believers* (God's elect), in contradistinction from '*the world of the ungodly*.'"[4]

God's Choice

Pink was attempting to make the crucial point that God is sovereign in the exercise of His love. The gist of his argument is certainly valid: it is folly to think that God loves all alike, or that He is compelled by some rule of fairness to love everyone equally. Scripture teaches us that God loves because He chooses to love (Deuteronomy 7:6–7), because He is loving—because He is love (1 John 4:8)—not because

He is under some obligation to love everyone the same. Nothing but God's own sovereign good pleasure compels Him to love sinners. Nothing but His own sovereign will governs His love. This has to be true, since there is certainly nothing in any sinner worthy of even the smallest degree of divine love.

Unfortunately, Pink took the corollary too far. The fact that some sinners are not elected to salvation is no proof that God's attitude toward them is utterly devoid of sincere love. We know from Scripture that God is compassionate, kind, generous, and good even to the most stubborn sinners. Who can deny that these mercies flow out of God's boundless love? Yet it is evident that they are showered even on unrepentant sinners. According to Paul, for example, the knowledge of divine goodness and forbearance and patience ought to lead sinners to repentance (Romans 2:4). Yet the apostle acknowledged that many who are the recipients of these expressions of divine love spurn them and thereby store up wrath for themselves in the day of wrath (v. 5). The hardness of the sinful human heart is the only reason people persist in their sin, despite God's goodness to them. Is God therefore insincere when He pours forth mercies calling them to repentance? And how can anyone conclude that God's real attitude toward those who reject His mercies is nothing but sheer hatred?

I want to acknowledge, however, that explaining God's love toward the reprobate is not as simple as most modern evangelicals want to make it. Clearly there is a sense in which the psalmist's expression, "I hate the assembly of evildoers" (Psalm 26:5 NASB), is a reflection of the mind of God. "Do I not hate those who hate You, O LORD? And do I not loathe those who rise up against You? I hate them with the utmost hatred; they have become my enemies" (Psalm 139:21–22 NASB). Such hatred as the psalmist expressed is a virtue, and we have every reason to conclude that it is a hatred God Himself shares. After all, He *did* say, "I have hated Esau" (Malachi 1:3 NASB; see Romans 9:13). The context reveals God was speaking of a *whole race* of wicked people. So there is a true and real sense in which Scripture teaches that God hates the wicked.

Eternal Destination

Many try to dodge the difficulty this poses by suggesting that God hates the sin, not the sinner. Why, then, does God condemn the sinner and consign the person—not merely the sin—to eternal hell? Clearly we cannot sweep the severity of this truth away by denying God's hatred for the wicked. Nor should we imagine that such hatred is any kind of blemish on the character of God. It is a holy hatred. It is perfectly consistent with His spotless, unapproach-able, incomprehensible holiness.

We must remember that God is Lord of the universe, and He can do whatever He wants.

CHAPTER 2

LORD IN OUR LIVES

Although God is Lord over us, we must submit to Him and to His sovereignty in our lives.

To give glory to Christ, we must confess Him as Lord. That's a part of salvation, not a subsequent act. Salvation is a matter of confessing that Christ is God and, therefore, that He is sovereign in your life.

If you have never confessed Jesus Christ as Lord, you have no capacity to live for His glory. You cannot say, "I deny Christ. He is not my Savior or Lord," and then expect to glorify God. If you dishonor the Son, you dishonor the Father (John 5:23). So salvation is the necessary beginning for glorifying God and, therefore, for spiritual growth. You cannot grow until you are born.

RESPONSE TO THE GOSPEL

In Matthew 13, the Lord began with a discussion of a sower and seed. In verses 4–8, the sower cast his seeds with these results:

immediately sprang up because they had no depth of earth. But when the sun was up they were scorched, and because they had no root they withered away. And some fell among thorns, and the thorns sprang up and choked them. But others fell on good ground and yielded a crop: some a hundredfold, some sixty, some thirty.

This story tells us that in response to the preaching of the gospel, there are at least four different possible results. And only one of them is genuine reception, producing righteousness.

The lesson appears once more, beginning in Matthew 13:47–50:

Again, the kingdom of heaven is like a dragnet that was cast into the sea and gathered some of every kind, which, when it was full, they drew to shore; and they sat down and gathered the good into vessels, but threw the bad away. So it will be at the end of the age. The angels will come forth, separate the wicked from among the just, and cast them into the furnace of fire. There will be wailing and gnashing of teeth.

The church is a net that pulls in every kind of person, good and bad. And one day, angels will separate the true followers from the false. Time and again in the New Testament, the Lord brought up the idea of identifying the true disciples as well as the pretenders. So Matthew 10:38–39 is consistent with the message as it occurs throughout Scripture.

I'm notorious in some circles for being "too inflexible" in defining what does and does not characterize a true follower of Christ. Here's the only truth: the supreme authority of God's revelations in Scripture. Nothing else counts. This deep loyalty to the truth I absorbed to a large extent from Dr. Charles Fineberg, a converted Jew, an immense intellect, and the dean of Talbot Seminary, where I graduated. He was my mentor, had a high view of Scripture, and taught me to have the same.

Even more so, my father taught me the truth of Scripture. He was a great teacher and a Bible expositor, one who allowed the Word of God to frame his understanding of salvation. He got the story straight and preached it right. There was never anything shallow about his ministry. And he taught me there's never any doubt about what makes true salvation and discipleship.

THE MARK OF CHRIST

The apostle Paul made a paradoxical statement in Romans 9:6 when he said, "They are not all Israel who are of Israel." In other words, all who are outwardly Jews are not inwardly Jews. All who are outwardly identified as the people of God are not inwardly the people of God. And we could say, then, that all disciples are not disciples; all apparent followers of Jesus are not actual followers of Jesus. We could even say that all the church, as we see it, is not the church. Matthew 10 describes the hallmarks of a genuine disciple. The message there is a message, first of all, about genuineness, and second, a message about impact: Who is a real disciple? How does he impact the world? How does the world impact him?

The first characteristic of a genuine disciple is that he is like his Lord. He bears the character of Christ. That's why in Acts 11:26 people called the believers Christians: *Christiani*—"iani" means "belonging to the party of." They were little Christs; they manifested His character and bore the marks of His life in them. A true Christian not only wears the name of Christ, but he demonstrates the virtue of Christ. Matthew 10:24–25 declares a self-evident axiom: "A disciple is not above his teacher, nor a servant above his master. It is enough for a disciple that he be like his teacher, and a servant like his master." People become like those whose influence dominates them.

Jesus repeated this truism in Luke 6:40, saying, "A disciple is not above his teacher, but everyone who is perfectly trained will be like his teacher." Beyond the discipling of the Spirit of Christ in us is the reality that He Himself has come to live in us, so that we can say with Paul, "It is no longer I who live, but Christ lives in me" (Galatians 2:20). A true disciple acts like Christ. Of course, there'll be lapses because of our humanness, but nonetheless there will be evidence of Christlikeness in the life of a true believer.

If we're true disciples, we have Jesus' hallmark on us; He is our maker. He is our life. Paul wonderfully affirmed this in 2 Corinthians 5:17: "Therefore, if anyone is in Christ, he is a new creation; old things have passed away; behold, all things have become new." That newness must be manifest.

The Character of Christ

The second and consequential characteristic of true disciples is that if we are like Christ, other people will respond to us as they did Christ. Matthew 10:25 continues: "If they have called the master of the house Beelzebub, how much more will they call those of his household!" Being a genuine Christian means to exhibit the character of Christ and, thus, to be treated as He was treated. When we move into the world with Christlike character, the world will react to us the way it reacted to Him. That was Jesus' message in John 15:20 when He said, "'A servant [some translations read "slave"] is not greater than his master.' If they persecuted Me, they will also persecute you.

If they kept [obeyed] My word, they will keep yours also." If you are genuine in your identification with Christ, you can expect the world that rejects Christ to reject you.

Loyalty to Christ

Still, it is also characteristic of a true disciple of Jesus that he is not afraid of the world. Matthew 10:28 says, "And do not fear those who kill the body but cannot kill the soul. But rather fear Him who is able to destroy both soul and body in hell." There's no reason to be afraid, because, as a follower of Jesus, you know you will happily trade whatever perils you face in this world for the riches of your reward in the eternal world to come. Disciples joyfully "speak in the light" and "preach on the housetops" (v. 27), untroubled by any rebuke or threat. Furthermore, there's no reason to fear what happens here, because not even a sparrow falls (actually the word means "hops") to the ground outside of God's will. "But the very hairs of your head are all numbered. Do not fear therefore; you are of more value than many sparrows" (vv. 30–31).

When the world is hostile and persecuting, when the world moves against him and ostracizes or alienates him, a true disciple is not afraid, because he has utterly and totally given himself over to the lordship of Christ, confident in His care no matter what, even against the hostility of the world. Another characteristic of discipleship is that a true disciple is loyal to his Lord. In verse 32, Jesus told us, "Therefore whoever confesses Me before men, him I will also confess before My Father who is in heaven." When the heat is on, when the pressure and the persecution are bearing down and the world is attacking, the true believer will openly confess Christ. He won't bail out. He won't deny his faith. He won't recant. He'll stand up and proclaim Christ, no matter what the circumstances. He'll go to prison and even face execution before he will deny his Lord.

Someone will say, "What about Peter? He was a real disciple, but he denied his Lord." It's true. He did. But it was before the Holy Spirit came to live in him. After that, he never again was disloyal. He died for being loyal to Christ: crucified upside down, as he requested, because he said he was not worthy to die like his Lord. Such loyalty marks the ones whom Christ will confess belong to Him.

The Sword of Christ

A central characteristic of a true disciple—and in some ways, almost an unbelievable one, because it goes so radically against our natural longings—is a willingness to forsake family if necessary. In Matthew 10:34, which we looked at earlier, Jesus said, "Do not think that I came to bring peace on earth. I did not come to bring peace but a sword." This is a most dramatic statement. He was saying, "Now, some of you who are real followers will confess Me when you're brought to the tribunals and the courts of men, and even in the course of day-to-day life. Others of you will deny Me, because it isn't that important to you, and you'll save your necks and your reputations. And that just proves that I have come to bring a sword. I cause divisions. I force people to decisions that separate one from another."

The very fact that some confess Christ and some deny Christ indicates that His coming causes divisions. Jesus didn't deny that stark reality, He built on it. The Jews knew from the Old Testament that when the Messiah came, He was coming to bring peace. Isaiah prophesied that He would be the Prince of Peace (Isaiah 9:6). Under His reign, warring factions would beat their swords into plowshares and their spears into pruning hooks (Isaiah 2:4). War—even the knowledge of war—would pass away.

They knew the marvelous words of hope in Psalm 72:3, 7 as it talks of the kingdom: "The mountains will bring peace to the people . . . / . . . In His days the righteous shall flourish, / And abundance of peace, / Until the moon is no more." There would be no war, only peace.

As Jesus was speaking to the disciples, they had already begun to experience the peace in their hearts that came just from being with Him. And they may have been anticipating that this bliss would extend to everybody. The disciples may have imagined they would go out to preach, and the whole world would fall at their feet because the Messiah, the Prince of Peace they had awaited for so long, had finally arrived. They were experiencing this euphoria of being with Him, confident that everybody else would respond the same way and Christ's wonderful, peaceful kingdom was just around the corner.

But that wasn't the true picture. So the Lord told them, "Don't be under any illusions about My coming now to bring peace. I've come not to send peace, but a sword." This idea expressed here sounds as if the Lord's intention for coming was to bring conflict. Consequences are often expressed as if they were intentions, for in the ultimate sovereignty of God, they are. But here, Jesus described the direct result of His coming as if it were His deliberate intention. And this is a paradox, in a sense. The Lord was saying, "On the one hand, I'm a prince of peace, but on the other hand, there's going to be war, represented by a sword." The Old Testament represented both of these points of view. It saw the fracturing, the breaking asunder. Micah 7:6 describes the Lord's coming this way: "For son dishonors father, / Daughter rises against her mother, / Daughter-in-law against her mother-in-law; / A man's enemies are the men of his own household." Our Lord almost directly quoted that in Matthew 10.

21

The Old Testament saw the Messiah as a king of peace, but it also saw a potential for division in His coming because some would accept Him, and others, even in the same family, would reject Him. The Jews also believed this division would take place. In some of the rabbinical writings, we find this statement: "In the period when the Son of David shall come, a daughter will rise up against her mother, a daughter-in-law against her mother-in-law. The son despises his father, the daughter rebels against the mother, the daughter-in-law against the mother-in-law, and a man's enemies are they of his own household."

It's as if Jesus was saying there will be a division *for the moment.* The intervention of God in history through the incarnation of Christ was going to split and fracture the world into parties that would pit themselves against one another. So don't be under any illusion as a disciple to think the whole world is going to fall at your feet. You're going to rush home and tell everybody you've become a Christian? You're going to shout the news at school, and everybody's going to line up to join you? It's not going to happen.

THE BIGGEST RIFT

Martin Luther said, "If our gospel were received in peace, it wouldn't be the true gospel." In a real sense,

Matthew 10:34 is paradoxical because we should expect the Lord to bring peace. After all, John the Baptist was His herald, and he talked about peace. When the angels proclaimed His birth, they said, "Peace on earth." And Jesus, in John 14:27, said, "My peace I give to you."

In at least three places in the book of Romans, Paul talked about the peace that God has given us (5:1; 8:6; 14:17). It's true that there is peace in the heart of the one who believes, but as far as the world is concerned, there's nothing but division. Yes, He brought the peace of God to the heart of a believer, and someday there will be a kingdom of peace. The Old Testament didn't always make a clear distinction between the First Coming and the Second Coming. The first brought a sword; the second will bring the ultimate peace.

It is true that the First Coming brought a partial peace, the peace that enters the hearts of those who believe. But the Lord warned the disciples, "You just remember this as you go out: You're going to cause division. You're going to cause a rending and a splitting apart."

The gospel does that. It is the refiner's fire that consumes. It brings the shepherd's separation of the sheep and the goats. It brings the husbandman's fan when he throws the grain into the air and the chaff is blown away. The entrance of Christ splits and tears apart. If Christ had never come, the earth would have gone on in unity, doomed to hell. But when He came, a war broke out.

In Luke 12, we see something of this. In verse 49, Jesus said, "I came to send fire on the earth, and how I wish it were already kindled!" Verse 51: "Do you suppose that I came to give peace on earth? I tell you, not at all, but rather division." He came to bring a sword, not peace, in the sense that He came to set members of a family against each other. He was saying that if you're a true disciple, you'll be willing to create a division in your own home. That goes against all of our instincts because we want peace in our homes more than anywhere else. That's our refuge, that's where the people we love the most and know the best live. We don't want to be at odds with them. But when we commit ourselves to Jesus Christ, we'll be true to Him, even if it destroys our homes, our neighborhoods, our cities, or our nation. If that's the price, we'll pay it.

Jesus expressed the severity of this severance in the phrase in Matthew 10:35: "For I have come to 'set a man against his father.'" Some translations have "set a man at variance against his own father." The Greek term for "at variance" or "set against" is a rare one, used only here in the New Testament. It means to cut asunder. Jesus was saying, "I will cut a man off totally from his father, and all these other relatives from each other. I'll fracture families every way possible."

This is the worst rending that can happen. It's not so bad when you're at odds with your neighbor, your boss, your friend, or your society, but when it gets into the family, and your commitment to Jesus Christ means that you are severed from your relatives, that's where it really begins to rub. Your commitment to Christ goes against your love and need for them.

Your commitment goes against the harmony with which you desire to live. Being a Christian and following Jesus Christ may mean you create a division in your own home. But that's the mark of a true disciple. Clinging to Christ often means letting go of family members who reject you because you won't reject the gospel. That's especially true in Jewish families, as well as those in false religions.

This is a hard standard, and many people decide it's too much of a sacrifice. Some wives will not come to Christ for fear of separation from their husbands. Some husbands will not come to Christ for fear of separation from their wives. Children may not come to Christ for fear of their fathers or mothers, and vice versa. People will not take a stand for Christ because they want to maintain that family harmony. But Jesus said the true disciple will turn from his family, if he is forced to make a choice. This is part of self-denial, accepting gladly the high cost of following Jesus to receive His infinite blessings for time and eternity.

A HIGHER LOVE

Family love is strong, surely the tightest human bond. But it doesn't have the power that love for Christ has. It is so strong that it sometimes cuts the family bond. One young lady from a totally pagan family said she had become a Christian and, as a result, her father, whom she greatly loved, refused to speak to her either in person or on the phone; he would hang up on her. She said, "I would think he'd be happy that I'm not an alcoholic, I'm not a drug addict, I'm not a criminal, and that I haven't been in some terrible accident, crippled, or injured. I've never had such joy in my life as I have now as a Christian, and because of my love for Christ he won't talk to me." That's because of the sword.

The same sword fell between Cain and Abel. Abel was a righteous man, Cain was an unrighteous man, and the cleavage was so great that Cain couldn't stand it—so he murdered his brother.

First Corinthians 7 tells us how that sword comes right into a Christian marriage. If you have an unbelieving wife, and she wants to stay with you, don't divorce her. If you have an unbelieving husband who wants to stay with you, then let him stay, because a certain sanctifying occurs. That is, the blessing that falls on the believer from God splashes onto the unbelieving partner in a temporal way. "But if the unbeliever departs, let him depart; a brother or sister is not under bondage in such cases. But God has called us to peace" (v. 15). That's the other side of it. Once the sword falls, then God has called us to peace, and if the unbeliever wants out, let him out.

Becoming a Christian means being sick of your sin, longing for forgiveness and rescue from present evil and future hell, and affirming your commitment to the lordship of Christ to the point where you are willing to forsake everything. I've said it before and I'll say it again: it isn't just holding up your hand or walking down an aisle and saying, "I love Jesus." It is not easy, it is not user-friendly or seeker-sensitive; it isn't a rosy, perfect world where Jesus gives you whatever you want. It is hard, it is sacrificial, and it supersedes everything. The manifestation of true faith is a commitment that no influence can sway. Of course you love your family, your children, your parents, and your husband or wife. But if you're a real disciple, your commitment to the salvation found only in Christ is so deep, profound, and far-reaching that you will say no, if need be, to those you love for the cause of Christ.

I pray to God I never have to make that decision, but I might. You may have had to make that choice because you confessed Jesus Christ, and it has been a burden on your family. But that's the way we prove the reality of our conversion. The one who says, "I'm not willing to make that sacrifice" isn't genuine. "He who loves father or mother more than Me," said Jesus in Matthew 10:37, "is not worthy of Me." You can't be His disciple and receive His salvation if your family means more to you than He does.

WILLING TO DIE

Only one thing is even more apt than the family to rob Christ of His rightful place in the heart of an individual, and that is the love of his own life. Sure, you might be willing to take Christ and lose your family, but would you be willing to take Christ and lose your life?

Now we're getting serious about who is a Christian.

THE MOTIVE OF THE CHURCH

If you were to survey a group of people and ask them to name the primary purpose of the church, you would probably get a variety of answers.

Some might suggest that the church is a place to form friendships with godly people. It's where believers strengthen each other in faith and where love is cultivated and shared.

Others might suggest that the mission of the church is teaching the Word, training believers for various responsibilities, and instructing children and young people with the purpose of helping them mature in Christ.

Still others might say that another purpose of the church is to praise God. The church is a community of praise that exalts God for who He is and what He has done. Some would suggest that since praise is the central activity of heaven, it must also be the primary responsibility of those on earth.

But as important as fellowship, teaching, and praise are, the primary motive of the church is to glorify God. The apostle Paul described salvation as being "to the praise of the glory of His grace" (Ephesians 1:6).

Our Mission

God loved a lost world and sought to win sinners to Himself for His own glory—*"God was in Christ reconciling the world unto himself"* (2 Corinthians 5:19 KJV). Christ came into the world out of love and sought to win sinners for the Father's glory. As believers we also are to go to the world in love and to seek to reach the lost for the glory of God. Thus our mission is the same as God's.

We are an extension of the ministry of God the Father and Son in receiving glory by the salvation of lost sinners. Jesus said, "As thou hast sent me into the world, even so have I also sent them into the world" (John 17:18 KJV). "As" conveys intention. As the Father sent the Son into the unredeemed world, so the Son has sent believers. Wonder of wonders, we have the privilege of participating in Jesus Christ's mission to a lost world!

Availability

"Here am I! Send me," answered Isaiah (Isaiah 6:8).

God desires a heart that is available at the appointed place and time to hear His orders. He also desires a heart full of true worship. The believer's whole affection and mind is to be set on Christ. All his goals are directed toward Him. He is his all in all.

So are you available? Are you a worshipper? Is your intent and purpose in life focused on the Person of Christ? Having those attitudes means being controlled by the Holy Spirit, who is the only One who can cause you to call Jesus Lord (1 Corinthians 12:3). All your possessions, time, energy, talent, and gifts are to be under His control.

That also means being centered on the Word because the Word is where Christ is seen. You gaze at His glory in the Word. As Christ came into the world to give His life to bring people to Himself, so you must do likewise.

All Authority

"All authority has been given to Me in heaven and on earth" (Matthew 28:18)—Jesus made this statement just before issuing the Great Commission. To "make disciples of all the nations," He had to establish His divine authority to give it. Otherwise, the command would have seemed impossible to fulfill.

As the disciples followed Jesus for three and a half years, they learned much about His authority. He showed them that He had authority over sickness (Matthew 4:23) and death (John 11:43–44). He gave His disciples the same power He had to overcome disease and demons (Matthew 10:1). He established that He had the authority to forgive sins (Matthew 9:6) and judge all men (John 5:25–29). And He proved that He had the authority to lay down His life and take it up again (John 10:18).

Submission to that absolute authority of Christ is not an option—it is your supreme obligation.

The Lost Sheep

At the beginning of the parable of the lost sheep, Jesus asks, "What man of you, having a hundred sheep, if he loses one of them, does not leave the ninety-nine in the wilderness, and go after the one which is lost until he finds it?" (Luke 15:4). Jesus' point is that any shepherd would seek a lost sheep, for it is not only a matter of duty but also of affection.

After finding the one sheep, the shepherd in this parable went home and invited people over to celebrate with him. The shepherd's joy was so great he had to share it.

We know that "there will be more joy in heaven over one sinner who repents than over ninety-nine just persons who need no repentance" (Luke 15:7). This verse is the conclusion to the parable and a hope for Christians today. Just as a shepherd rejoices over the lost sheep, our Great Shepherd rejoices over the repentant sinner, for He has found His lost sheep.

Renewing Our Passion

"Jesus went about all the cities and villages, teaching in their synagogues, preaching the gospel of the kingdom" (Matthew 9:35).

Everything worthwhile in life is the result of someone's passion. Significant events of human history are the result of a deep and consuming desire to see goals fulfilled. The consuming desire of believers should be to see the gospel reach the world. However, we live in an age that tends to dull our sharpness. Our culture obscures legitimate goals and would rob our faith of its fiery power if given the chance.

Indeed, some Christians are a cold bath for the fiery heart. They just don't understand someone with a passionate concern about a spiritual enterprise, because spiritual passion is not the norm. The norm is not to let Christianity disrupt your lifestyle. If you follow that, your spiritual temperature will drop and you'll become apathetic.

We all need to ask ourselves, *Where is our burden for evangelism? Why isn't evangelism the church's central function? Is the church only a self-indulgent activity center, content with comfort and prosperity?*

EXAMPLES OF PASSION

"He Himself gave some to be apostles, some prophets, some evangelists, and some pastors and teachers" (Ephesians 4:11).

It was said that John Wesley did more for England than her armies and navies. He lived meagerly, having given away thousands of dollars in his lifetime. Abused and maligned, he left his reputation and soul in the hands of God. It has been estimated he traveled 225 thousand miles on foot and horseback and preached twenty-four hundred sermons. Much of the established church despised him, but he brought fire into her cold heart. He had the reputation of being out of breath pursuing souls.

Ordained at twenty-two, George Whitefield began preaching with tremendous eloquence and effect. His power came from his passion for souls, and he used every one of his God-given abilities to lead men to Christ. He crossed the Atlantic thirteen times and preached thousands of sermons. His gravestone reads that he was a soldier of the cross, humble, devout, and ardent, preferring the honor of Christ to his own interest, reputation, or life.

Though these men are wonderful examples, the perfect example of one with passion for the lost is Christ.

CHAPTER 3

DAILY SUBMISSION

Life of EASE

Submitting to Christ as Lord must be a day-by-day experience, regardless of our feelings or the cost.

Theodore Roosevelt once said, "There has never yet been a man who led a life of ease, whose name is worth remembering." Certainly when the Lord calls us to be His disciples, He does not call us to a life of ease. A missionary whose story has influenced my life greatly is a man named Henry Martyn. After a long and difficult life of Christian service in India, he announced he was going to go to Persia (modern Iran), because God had laid it upon his heart to translate the New Testament and the Psalms into the Persian language. By then he was an old man. People told him that if he stayed in India, he would die from the heat, and that Persia was hotter than India. But he went nonetheless.

There he studied the Persian language and then translated the entire New Testament and Psalms in nine months. Then he learned that he couldn't print or circulate them until he received the Shah's permission. He traveled six hundred miles to Tehran; there he was denied permission to see the Shah. He turned around and made a four-hundred-mile trip to find the British ambassador, who gave him the proper letters of introduction and sent him the four hundred miles back to Tehran. This was in 1812, and Martyn made the whole trip on the back of a mule, traveling at night and resting by day, protected from the sweltering desert sun by nothing but a strip of canvas.

He finally arrived back in Tehran, was received by the Shah, and secured permission for the Scriptures to be printed and circulated in Persia. Ten days later he died. But shortly before his death, he had written this statement in his diary: "I sat in the orchard, and thought, with sweet comfort and peace, of my God; in solitude my Company, my Friend, and Comforter."

He certainly did not live a life of ease, but it was a life worth remembering. And he's one of many God used to turn redemptive history.

Bound up in the spirit of Henry Martyn is the key to genuine discipleship, which is to be so utterly consumed with the cause that you have no thought for your own life. Verses 38–39 of Matthew 10 highlight this aspect of serving Christ: "And he who does not take his cross and follow after Me is not worthy of Me. He who finds his life will lose it, and he who loses his life for My sake will find it."

Many people claim to follow Jesus. Many people claim to be His disciples, and many always have. But in these verses of Matthew, our Lord pointed to the proof of genuineness. This is the mark of a real follower of Christ.

The message of genuineness is one the Lord spoke about again and again. But it seems to be one that today's Christian church often overlooks. The Lord repeatedly compared true disciples against false, the real against the fake. For Him, this was an essential matter. And so He talked frequently about genuine salvation as opposed to a facade of salvation.

In Matthew alone, this is a constant issue. In chapter 5, verse 20, His first sermon recorded in the New Testament, our Lord said this: "For I say to you, that unless your righteousness exceeds the righteousness of the scribes and Pharisees, you will by no means enter the kingdom of heaven." There is the genuine, perfect righteousness of Christ that is imputed to each believer (Romans 4:5; Philippians 3:9; 2 Corinthians 5:21), and there is a false righteousness of men. And unless you have the real thing, you'll not enter the kingdom. Jesus was focusing here on the sham righteousness of the Pharisees. We see the same warning in Matthew 7, where Jesus spoke of that narrow gate that only a few people ever find. There are two roads that seem to go to God, but one leads to life, the other to destruction. Later in that same sermon, Jesus concluded with the parable of the man who built his house on sinking sand while his neighbor built on solid rock.

FOLLOWING DAILY

Matthew 10:38 says, "And he who does not take his cross and follow after Me is not worthy of Me." We're back to that cross again. The whole point of this section of biblical text is to stress one incredible idea: total self-denial to the point of death.

The Lord was really zeroing in on what a true believer was. Unless you're willing to take up your cross and follow Him, you aren't truly a follower. No doubt you've heard a zillion devotionals on "taking up your cross." But your cross isn't your broken-down car or your unappreciative spouse. When Jesus told His listeners to take up their crosses, it meant only one thing to them. It meant willingly facing the possibility of death for His sake.

Eleven of the twelve apostles (all except Judas) were from Galilee, where another Judas, Judas of Galilee, had recently led an insurrection. He gathered a force to throw the Romans out, but the Romans won. They crushed Judas and his insurrection. The Roman general, Varus, wanting to teach the Jews a lesson, crucified more than two thousand of them. He put their crosses up and down all the roads of Galilee, so people saw them everywhere they traveled. Every crucified Jew had carried his own crossbeam as he marched to death by crucifixion.

These Galileans had seen all of that, and Jesus

was talking to them in a historical context, saying they needed to be willing to face such a consequence rather than deny Him. Jesus was saying that to follow Him, we must be willing to go through the most horrific death imaginable.

Committing your life to follow Jesus Christ means you would not only forsake your family; if need be, you'd give your life. The world should never intimidate you, and you must be willing to confess Christ in the most hostile environment.

The disciples understood that to "take up the cross" meant a willingness to die any death. It meant abandoning self to the lordship of Christ. The love of Christ has to overrule both the powerful appeal of family love and the more powerful instinct of self-preservation.

As we heard in other texts, again Jesus added this rich thought in Matthew 10:39: "He who finds his life will lose it, and he who loses his life for My sake will find it." Whoever protects his physical safety by denying Christ under pressure will lose his eternal soul. But if you're willing to lose your life for Christ's sake, you'll find eternal life in the end. Being a martyr doesn't save you. If you're a genuine Christian, though, you value nothing so much that you will turn away from Christ, knowing that the one who confesses Jesus Christ and dies for Him is far better off than the apostate who escapes death by denying Christ and receives eternal damnation. Officials brought John Bunyan before the magistrates when they put him in prison, and he said, "Sir, the law of Christ hath provided two ways of obeying: The one to do that which I in my conscience do believe I am bound to do, actively; and where I cannot obey it actively, there I am willing to lie down and suffer what they shall do unto me."

He was right. If you serve Christ actively and aggressively, you pay the price. But it is better to lose everything here—better to lose your ease and comfort, to be hassled and intimidated, badgered by the world; better even to lose your family, to lose your life—than to forsake Jesus Christ. And thank God, it isn't that we will necessarily have to make all these sacrifices, but if we're really His, if it comes to that, we will do it. Salvation in Christ is that precious.

THE JOY OF BELIEVING

These last two sections on persecution and suffering are characteristics of a true believer. Seen in this light, the truth about being a disciple seems filled with sacrifice and foreboding. Does being a Christian mean you're destined to face the world's harassment, having to confess before men, forsaking your family, and giving your life? Don't we do anything but create problems in the world?

Of course we do. A true disciple receives his due reward. As well as creating war, strife, division, separation, and friction, we do have a positive effect. We are the destiny-determiners in the world. When we bring down the sword that separates, on the one hand are the unbelievers, but on the other hand are the *believers*. And when we preach, live, and give our testimonies, thank God some respond in genuine repentance and self-denying faith. Everything is as bright for them as it is dark for the nonbelievers. Not everyone is going to refuse the message of the disciple. Some are going to believe and receive their Lord. And since we have limited ability to reward their faith, the Lord will do it for us.

Matthew 10:40 says, "He who receives you receives Me, and he who receives Me receives Him who sent Me." Let me tell you what's in the word *receive* here. When you represent Jesus Christ and proclaim His Word, the people who believe it are the ones who receive you. It is a full receiving, in that they accept you and your message. And the ones who receive you are also receiving the Lord. In turn, the ones receiving the Lord are receiving the one who sent the Lord. That means you become an agency of men's receiving God Himself. Wow! What greater privilege could we imagine?

On the one hand, you create this antagonism by standing fast in the faith; then, on the other hand, you create this marvelous reality that people receive God through you. Every time somebody says to me, "You know, I was saved when you preached," or "I received Christ when you told me the gospel," I am thrilled beyond the ability to express it. I didn't save anybody, but God used me as His instrument to forgive and reconcile those people to Himself forever.

It's pretty overwhelming to grasp that God has used a frail, human, clay pot as His means of saving others. But the reward goes even beyond that. Look at Matthew 10:41: "He who receives a prophet in the name of a prophet shall receive a prophet's reward. And he who receives a righteous man in the name of a righteous man shall receive a righteous man's reward." That's a tremendous divine principle. By the way, a prophet is what he *says*, and a righteous man is what he *is*, so the two really speak of the same individual. A true disciple lives what he says. He speaks the gospel truth, and he lives righteously. When you go out representing God by your life and your lips, by your speaking and your living, those who receive you will receive the reward that you receive. This could be true of a pastor, a teacher, a missionary, an evangelist, or anyone who represents Christ; the one who receives that one will share that one's reward. If the Lord gives me a reward for proclaiming to you, He'll give you the same reward for receiving what I proclaim. We all share.

You want to be a blessing in the world? Then confess Christ before men! Stand up boldly, and don't mitigate your testimony; don't be ashamed of Christ. Don't water down the truth. And let your life become the source of their reward. Then a disciple is a person who determines destiny. Even the least of us shares with the greatest of us in what God does in blessing us.

BRIDGE BUILDERS

There was a lad in a country village who, after a great struggle, reached the ministry. All through his days of study, a cobbler in the village had helped him. He was a simple man but well read, and he loved God with all his heart.

In time, the young lad he had helped became licensed to preach, and on the day of his ordination, the cobbler said to him, "Young man, I always had in my heart the desire to be a minister of the gospel, but the circumstances of my life never made it possible. You are doing what was always my dream, but never reality. I want you to promise me one thing. I want you to let me make you a pair of shoes for nothing, and I want you to wear them in the pulpit when you preach. Then I'll feel you are preaching the gospel I always wanted to preach, standing in my shoes."

Because of whom he represents, you will receive a disciple no matter how meager or unassuming he is. And in that true receiving, you will receive the message he brings of the Savior and the Father, and you will embrace the whole of the blessedness of God's eternal gifts to those who are His own. Being a disciple of Jesus Christ is pretty fantastic. You become the source of conflict for some of the world, and the source of blessing for others. But you and I who are the disciples of Christ, we draw the lines. I pray we'll always be willing to follow the lordship of Christ at any price, in order that some may be antagonized, and some may be blessed.

In the depths of winter, Napoleon's army was retreating from its invasion of Russia. The army was pressed on all sides and had to cross the Berezina River to escape. The Russians had destroyed all the bridges, and Napoleon ordered that a bridge be built across the river. The men nearest the water were the first to attempt to carry out the almost impossible task. Several were carried away by the furious rapids. Others drowned due to the cold and their exhaustion, but more came and the work proceeded as quickly as possible. Finally, the builders completed the bridge and emerged half-dead from the icy water. As a result of that incredible effort, the French army marched across the Berezina River in safety.[1]

That was an instance of heroic self-sacrifice. In

a similar way, Christ calls His disciples to give their lives to build bridges for others to cross into the presence of God. If you're a true disciple, you will be willing to do just that.

WHO IS A DISCIPLE?

A disciple is someone who confesses Christ as Lord and Savior, believes that God has raised Him from the dead, and is willing to declare that belief publicly through baptism. He is not some sort of "upper-level" Christian. You don't have to wait to become a disciple at some future time in your Christian life when you have reached a certain level of maturity. According to Matthew 28:19–20, a disciple is made at the moment of salvation.

Some claim that there are many Christians who are not disciples. They say that in order to be a disciple, one has to deny himself, take up his cross, and follow Christ. If one is not up to that level of commitment, they think, then he is not worthy to be Christ's disciple. But you cannot separate discipleship from conversion.

When someone is saved, he receives a submissive spirit that manifests itself by a willingness to make a public confession and obey whatever else Christ commands. Are you, then, a disciple?

A View to Obedience

You cannot be a disciple apart from a life of obedience and a desire to follow Christ as Lord. One of the most important ways we obey is by teaching others to obey His commands.

Regarding the Holy Spirit, Jesus said, "He will teach you all things, and bring to your remembrance all things that I said to you" (John 14:26). Through the Word of God, the Spirit has made that teaching available to every believer. And every believer is to submit himself to it in obedience.

Only a true convert will obey Christ. Only as you "present yourselves to God as being alive from the dead, and your members as instruments of righteousness to God" (Romans 6:13) do you exhibit obedient faith.

The End of Growth

Second Peter 3:18 commands believers to "grow in the grace and knowledge of our Lord and Savior Jesus Christ." Your response to this verse is either action or inaction. If you desire to mature in Christ, you will experience blessing, usefulness, and victory by following the biblical path of glorifying God. And as David discovered, you will also experience joy: "I have set the LORD always before me . . . Therefore my heart is glad" (Psalm 16:8–9).

The apostle John summed up the goal of spiritual

growth when he said, "Beloved, now we are children of God; and it has not yet been revealed what we shall be, but we know that when He is revealed, we shall be like Him, for we shall see Him as He is" (1 John 3:2). The growth process will end on the day that we see Jesus Christ and become like Him.

MATURITY IN SUFFERING

"May the God of all grace, who called us to His eternal glory by Christ Jesus, after you have suffered a while, perfect, establish, strengthen, and settle you" (1 Peter 5:10).

A Christian's call to glory necessitates walking the path of suffering. This verse explains why. Suffering is God's way of maturing His people spiritually. He is pleased when we patiently endure the suffering that comes our way. Suffering is a part of God's plan to prepare His people for glory.

The apostle Peter said this regarding the value of suffering: "You greatly rejoice, though now for a little while, if need be, you have been grieved by various trials, that the genuineness of your faith, being much more precious than gold that perishes, though it is tested by fire, may be found to praise, honor, and glory at the revelation of Jesus Christ" (1 Peter 1:6–7). God allows suffering as a validation of our faith. It also produces patience, though patience is a quality we won't need in eternity—there will be no reason for *im*patience there. But beyond those benefits, suffering increases our capacity to praise, honor, and glorify God—and that's something we will use throughout eternity.

Ready to Suffer

Peter reminds us that "since Christ suffered for us in the flesh, arm yourselves also with the same mind" (1 Peter 4:1).

One of the blessings of being a Christian is our identification with Christ and its resulting privileges. However, just so we won't take those blessings for granted, assuming that they will result in our being loved and respected by the world, God also allows us to suffer. In fact, the apostle Peter in his first epistle clearly shows that those most blessed in the faith suffer the most.

The Christian life is a call to glory through a journey of suffering. That's because those in Christ are inevitably at odds with their culture and society. All Satan-energized systems are actively at odds with the things of Christ. The apostle John said a person can't love both God and the world (1 John 2:15), and James said, "Whoever therefore wants to be a friend of the world makes himself an enemy of God" (James 4:4).

Called to Suffer

"For to this [suffering] you were called" (1 Peter 2:21). Though this verse seems to point out that we are called to suffer, it actually refers back to the last part of verse 20, which says, "When you do good and suffer, if you take it patiently, this is commendable before God." When Christians endure suffering with patience, it pleases God.

That shouldn't surprise us. Earlier in this chapter of 1 Peter, the apostle Peter states that Christians "are a chosen generation, a royal priesthood, a holy nation, His own special people, that you may proclaim the praises of Him who called you out of darkness into His marvelous light" (v. 9). Our dark world resents and is often hostile toward those who represent the Lord Jesus Christ. That resentment and hostility may be felt at certain times and places more than others, but it is always there to some extent as a part of the privilege of being His own.

WHAT DO YOU REALLY LOVE?

Apart from God, nothing could have been dearer to Abraham than his son Isaac. But that was the test: to find out whether he loved Isaac more than God. If we love God supremely, we will thank Him for what He is accomplishing through our trials and sufferings. But if we love ourselves more than God, we will question God's wisdom and become upset and bitter. If anything is dearer to us than God, then He must remove it for us to grow spiritually.

Jesus said, "If anyone comes to Me and does not hate his father and mother, wife and children, brothers and sisters, yes, and his own life also, he cannot be My disciple. And whoever does not bear his cross and come after Me cannot be My disciple" (Luke 14:26–27).

In this verse, Jesus was not indicating that we're to hate everyone. Rather He meant that if you do not love God to the degree that you willingly, if necessary, cut yourself off from your father, mother, spouse, children, brother, sister, or even your own life, then you don't love Him supremely. You must determine to do the will of God first and foremost, no matter what appeals others may make to you.

A LIVING HOPE

When God saved you and transformed you, He gave you "an inheritance incorruptible and undefiled and that does not fade away" (1 Peter 1:4), "a living hope" (v. 3). As a result, Christians can live in the hope of that eternal inheritance.

Why is this hope important? Unbelievers do not

trust Him, so they cannot hope in Him. But as a believer, you have seen that God has been faithful in your past and present and that gives you the hope that He will be faithful in the future. And that gives Him glory.

Simply put, God is glorified when you trust Him. He's glorified when you believe Him. And He is glorified when you hope in His future promise. The God who has given you such a great salvation is worthy of your hope.

RIGHT PRIORITIES

Here's a Lordship challenge: "Set your mind on things above, not on things on the earth" (Colossians 3:2).

Where are your priorities? Are you focused on things of this world, or on spiritual issues? Would the coming of Jesus Christ tomorrow mess up your plans? Unfortunately, many Christians hope He doesn't show up for a while.

What a sad commentary! If you would rather stay on earth than be in Christ's glorious home in heaven, then you don't love His appearing. It grieves God when we don't live in anticipation of His glorious presence and are more interested in the mundane passing things of this world.

Where is your heart? It's time to take a close look at your priorities. When you're truly grateful for the salvation God has given, then you're living in the hope of the fullness of that salvation yet to come. Make John's desire your own: "Even so, come, Lord Jesus" (Revelation 22:20).

GRIEVING OVER LOST SOULS

Through His tears, Jesus exclaimed about His beloved Jerusalem, "How often I wanted to gather your children together, as a hen gathers her chicks under her wings, but you were not willing!" (Matthew 23:37).

Jesus deeply cared for individuals. Our Lord brought Philip (John 1:43), Matthew (Matthew 9:9), and Peter and Andrew (Matthew 4:18–19) to faith with the call, "Follow Me." In John 4, He met a woman at a well and brought her to salvation. In Luke 19, He found Zaccheus, a tax collector, whom He led to a confession of sin, repentance, and faith. In John 3, He taught Nicodemus about the new birth. In Mark 10, He led blind Bartimaeus to believe in Him. In Mark 5, Jesus healed a demon-possessed man in the country of the Gerasenes. And Luke 23 tells of His brief yet poignant encounter with the thief on the cross (vv. 40–43); before committing Himself to God, Christ rescued him from eternal hell.

Jesus' heart grieved over the souls of lost men and women. In John 5:40, we see a glimpse of Christ's passion when He said, "You are not willing to come to Me that you may have life." There's a pensive quality to those words. Does your heart echo the affection of His speech?

The Model of Witnessing

Paul told the Corinthian believers, "Imitate me, just as I also imitate Christ" (1 Corinthians 11:1).

Christ is the perfect model to imitate in witnessing to others. First, He was available. Although there were times when He left the crowds, Jesus was regularly among the people, even when He was busy.

Second, He wasn't partial. Often Jesus was with common people, lepers, prostitutes, and tax collectors—those belonging to the lower classes socially and morally. But He also helped a Roman centurion, a man of dignity and stature (Matthew 8:5–13), and ministered to wealthy Jairus, whose daughter needed a miracle (Mark 5:22–24, 35–43). Jesus reflected the mind of God, who is no respecter of persons (Acts 10:34).

Third, He was sensitive to the pain of others. In Mark 5, a lady with a hemorrhage for twelve years reached out and touched Christ's garment. Jesus asked, "Who touched My garments?" (v. 30 NASB) out of concern for her.

Last, He secured a public confession from those who believed in Him, such as the blind man (John

9:1–41) and the Samaritan leper (Luke 17:11–19). Follow Christ's example as you witness to others.

Fishing for Men

Jesus said He would make His followers "fishers of men" (Matthew 4:19).

Fishermen in the first century used special tools for catching fish. One was a line and hook (Matthew 17:27). Another was a spear or possibly a type of harpoon (Job 41:26). A third was the dragnet (Matthew 13:47). It was sometimes over three hundred feet long and about eight feet wide. Fishermen buoyed up one side with corks and weighed down the other side with lead sinkers. Sometimes they stretched the net between two boats and rowed in a circle. They would then draw in ropes attached to the bottom of the net, trapping the fish (John 21:6).

In this verse, however, Jesus was referring to a casting net, which had a circular form (about fifteen feet in diameter) made of fine mesh and lead sinkers around the edge. Attaching a long piece of line to the center of the net, the fisherman would cast it into shallow water. He then would draw up the center of the net by its cord and wade into the water to secure the catch.

Just as the disciples caught a school of fish within the reaches of their circular net, the Lord wants His contemporary disciples to reach out to the men and women around us.

Catch the Tide

Jesus told the disciples, "Lift up your eyes and look at the fields, for they are already white for harvest" (John 4:35).

All believers are responsible to have a passion for the lost. John Harper had such a passion. He was a newly called pastor to the great Moody Memorial Church in Chicago in the early 1900s, but in 1912 he was a passenger on the ill-fated voyage of the *Titanic*.

Four years later, a young Scotsman rose up in a meeting and said he was a survivor of the *Titanic*. As he drifted in the water on a piece of wood, he encountered a man who was afloat on a piece of wreckage. The man pleaded for the Scotsman to receive Christ. The young Scotsman refused. The tide brought the man around again, and he asked if the Scotsman was saved yet. Shortly after, the man disappeared into the water, and the Scotsman decided to trust Christ as Savior. At the meeting he identified the man as John Harper—the young Scotsman was John Harper's last convert.

Can you be one of the John Harpers of this generation?

GLORY THROUGH SUFFERING

"For our light affliction, which is but for a moment, is working for us a far more exceeding and eternal weight of glory" (2 Corinthians 4:17).

Suffering not only makes us stronger now—it makes us able to endure with patience, increases our faith, teaches us to trust God, and leads us to depend on Christ and His Word—but also affects how we will function later. That's why Paul went on to say our focus isn't on today but the future: "We do not look at the things which are seen, but at the things which are not seen. For the things which are seen are temporary, but the things which are not seen are eternal" (v. 18).

The greater our endurance through suffering, the greater our eternal reward.

Identifying with Christ's Suffering

"It was fitting for Him, for whom are all things and by whom are all things, in bringing many sons to glory, to make the captain of their salvation perfect through sufferings" (Hebrews 2:10).

Christians can identify with their Master because like Him, they suffer to enter their glory. Christ said to the disciples on the road to Emmaus, "O foolish ones, and slow of heart to believe in all that the prophets have spoken! Ought not the Christ to have suffered these things and to enter into His glory?" (Luke 24:25–26). Our Lord had to explain that future glory required that He suffer. We should expect the same.

The path to glory for Christ was the path of unjust suffering. That's our path also. Jesus endured suffering with perfect patience and was exalted to the highest point of glory. He is our example of how to respond to suffering.

Christ's suffering on the cross is the focal point of the Christian faith. That's where His deity, humanity, work, and suffering are most clearly seen.

A Suffering Standard

Jesus was executed as a criminal on a cross. Yet He was guilty of no crime—no wrong, no trespass, no sin. He never had an evil thought or spoke an evil word. His was the most unjust execution ever perpetrated on a human being. Yet it shows us that though a person may be perfectly within the will of God—greatly loved and gifted, perfectly righteous and obedient—he may still experience unjust suffering. Like Jesus, you may be misunderstood, misrepresented, hated, persecuted, and even murdered. Yet you must follow His standard. "For such a High Priest was fitting for us, who is holy, harmless, undefiled, separate from sinners, and has become higher than the heavens" (Hebrews 7:26).

Follow Christ's Example

"Christ also suffered for us, leaving us an example, that you should follow His steps" (1 Peter 2:21).

Jesus gave us the ultimate example of suffering. The Greek word translated as "example" refers to a pattern that is placed under a piece of paper to be traced. Like children who learn their letters using tracing paper over a pattern, we are to trace our lives according to the pattern Christ laid down for us.

We follow His pattern by walking "in His steps." We are to walk in Christ's steps because His was a righteous walk. It was also a walk of unjust suffering, which is part of the walk of righteousness. Some suffer more than others, but if you truly want to follow after Christ, you will practice tracing His example.

Our Sinless Savior

"[Christ] committed no sin, nor was deceit found in His mouth; who, when He was reviled, did not revile in return" (1 Peter 2:22–23).

Jesus would have been prominent in Peter's mind when he wrote these verses because he personally witnessed Jesus' pain—though from afar. In spite of the severity of His pain, however, Christ committed no sin in word or deed.

Isaiah 53:9 says, "He had done no violence." "Violence" is translated as "lawlessness" in the Septuagint (the Greek version of the Hebrew Old Testament). The translators understood that "violence" referred to violence against God's law—or sin. In spite of the unjust treatment He had to endure, Christ did not and could not sin (1 Peter 1:19).

Isaiah 53:9 adds, "Nor was any deceit in His mouth." Sin usually first makes its appearance in us by what we say. In Jesus there was no sin, neither externally nor internally.

Jesus Christ, our Lord, is the perfect model of how we are to respond to unjust treatment because He endured far worse treatment than any person who will ever live, and yet never sinned.

CHAPTER 4

HOLY LIVING

WHAT IS SANCTIFICATION?

Sanctification is the continuous operation of the Holy Spirit in believers, making us holy by conforming our character, affections, and behavior to the image of Christ. Justification is a one-time event; sanctification is an ongoing *process*. Justification frees us from the *guilt* of sin, sanctification from the *pollution* of sin. As we are seeing, one is as much a necessary part of God's saving work as the other.

Note this crucial distinction: At justification we surrender the *principle* of sin and self-rule. In sanctification we relinquish the *practice* of specific sins as we mature in Christ. Total surrender to Christ's lordship does not mean that we make all of life's decisions as a prerequisite to conversion.[1] It does not demand that we give up all our sins before we can be justified. It means that when we trust Christ for salvation we settle the issue of who is in charge. At salvation we surrender to Christ in principle, but as Christians we will surrender in practice again and again. This practical outworking of His lordship is the process of sanctification.

There *is* an immediate aspect of sanctification that is simultaneous with justification: "Such were some of you; but you were washed, but you were sanctified, but you were justified in the name of the Lord Jesus Christ and in the Spirit of our God" (1 Corinthians 6:11 NASB). This once-for-all aspect of sanctification is undoubtedly what the apostle had in view when he addressed the Corinthians as "those who *have been* sanctified" (1 Corinthians 1:2 NASB, emphasis added). This initial, immediate aspect is sometimes referred to as "positional sanctification." But sanctification, unlike justification, is not a one-time, legal declaration. It is an experiential separation from sin that begins at salvation and continues in increasing degrees of practical holiness in one's life and behavior. Sanctification may be observable in greater or lesser degrees from believer to believer. But it is not optional, nor is it separable from the other aspects of our salvation.

Perhaps the writer to the Hebrews stated the necessity of practical sanctification most succinctly: "Pursue peace with all men, and the sanctification without which no one will see the Lord" (Hebrews 12:14 NASB). The context shows that verse is speaking of holy behavior, practical righteousness, not just a positional or forensic holiness (vv. 11, 12, 13, 15, 16).

The Power of Transformation

Further on, in Romans 12 of his letter to the church in Rome, Paul said, "I beseech you therefore, brethren, by the mercies of God, that you present your bodies a living sacrifice, holy, acceptable to God, which is your reasonable service. And do not be conformed to this world, but be transformed by the renewing of your mind" (vv. 1–2). As you study the Bible and understand its truths, it transforms your thinking. It will begin to wean you off worldly pleasures and cause you to desire godliness. It has the power to separate you from the world's system, pull you away from the love of worldly things, and plant in your heart a love for godly things. Paul called Scripture "the mind of Christ" (1 Corinthians 2:16) because in it is revealed what our Lord thinks. Whoever knows Scripture knows the Lord's thoughts on all that is revealed there.

TOWARD CHRISTLIKENESS

Scripture recognizes that believers are not perfect. We all fail to achieve God's standard, which is "Be holy, for I am holy" (1 Peter 1:16). Paul saw the sin in his own life, but refused to let it stop him from doing everything he could to overcome it: "Not that I have already attained, or am already perfected; but I press on, that I may lay hold of that for which Christ Jesus has also laid hold of me. Brethren, I do not count myself to have apprehended; but one thing I do, forgetting those things which are behind and reaching forward to those things which are ahead, I press toward the goal for the prize of the upward call of God in Christ Jesus" (Philippians 3:12–14). In other words, our own imperfection should spur us on toward the goal of complete Christlikeness. Sanctification is the process by which God—working in believers through the Holy Spirit—gradually moves us toward that goal.

It's a gradual transformation. In Romans 12:2, Paul wrote, "Do not be conformed to this world, but be transformed by the renewing of your mind." He also affirmed that sanctification does not end unless "we all come to the unity of the faith and of the knowledge of the Son of God, to a perfect man, to the measure of the stature of the fullness of Christ" (Ephesians 4:13).

The Bible clearly teaches that you can never attain such sinless perfection in this life. Proverbs 20:9 challenges us: "Who can say, 'I have made my heart clean, I am pure from my sin'?" The apostle John affirmed, "If we say that we have no sin, we deceive ourselves, and the truth is not in us" (1 John 1:8). Sanctification is never complete in this lifetime—that will happen only when we are glorified. The word *sanctify* comes from Hebrew and Greek words that mean "set apart." To be sanctified is to be set apart from sin. At conversion, all believers are released from sin's penalty and set apart unto God. Yet the process of separation from the power of sin in your life has just begun. As you grow in Christ, you become further separated from the influence of sin and more consecrated to God. The sanctification that takes place at conversion initiates a lifelong process of distancing yourself further and further from sin and coming gradually and steadily more into conformity with Christlike righteousness.

Maturing Christians never become self-justifying, smug, or satisfied with their progress. They do not pursue self-esteem; they seek instead to deal with their sin.

The more you become like Christ, the more sensitive you are to the remaining corruptions of the flesh. As you mature in godliness, your sins become both more painful and more obvious. The more you put away sin, the more you will notice sinful tendencies you need to eliminate. That is the paradox of sanctification: the holier you become, the more frustrated you will be by the stubborn remnants of your sin.

The apostle Paul vividly described his own anguish over this reality in Romans 7:21–24:

I find then the principle that evil is present in me, the one who wants to do good. For I joyfully concur with the law of God in the inner man, but I see a different law in the members of my body, waging war against the law of my mind and making me a prisoner of the law of sin which is in my members. Wretched man that I am! Who will set me free from the body of this death? (NASB)

Romans 7 poses a number of difficult challenges for Bible interpreters, but surely the most difficult question of all is how Paul could say those things *after* he wrote in chapter 6, "Our old self was crucified with Him, in order that our body of sin might be done away with, so that we would no longer be slaves to sin; for he who has died is freed from sin" (vv. 6–7 NASB). These are vital truths for the Christian to understand. They hold the formula for a healthy spiritual walk, and they give much practical insight into how we should battle sin in our own lives. In order to understand them better, we must go back into Romans 6. According to Dr. Warfield, Romans 6 "was written for no other purpose than to assert and demonstrate that justification and sanctification are indissolubly bound together."[2]

Or, in Paul's own imagery, dying with Christ (justification) and living with Christ (sanctification) are both necessary results of true faith. Those who think grace makes holiness optional are tragically deceived. Those who think they have experienced all the sanctification they need are equally deluded. Those who think self-esteem is more important than holiness are blind to the truth. If we would know God's principles for dealing with sin, we must understand that it is a life-and-death struggle to the end. To be content with good feelings about oneself is to be content with sin. More than 150 years ago a dutiful Christian mother explained the idea beautifully to her daughter, who was grieved by her own newly revealed sin. The words are a little old-fashioned, but the message is timeless:

> Before His influence was shed into your heart, you could see none of your faults. It was like coming into the parlor some cloudy morning. All the dust and litter of the room would not be visible. But let a bright ray of sunshine gleam in and how you would see every particle of dust! So the Holy Spirit has shined into your heart and you are astonished at what you see there. Do not doubt for a moment His power and His willingness to receive you. He will never leave you or forsake you. Here on earth, we'll never become sanctified no matter how earnestly we pursue it. But pursue it we will if we are truly born again, for God Himself guarantees our perseverance in righteousness: "May the God of peace Himself sanctify you completely; and may your

whole spirit, soul, and body be preserved blameless at the coming of our Lord Jesus Christ" (1 Thessalonians 5:23).

HOW DOES SANCTIFICATION WORK?

The word *sanctify* in Scripture comes from Hebrew and Greek words that mean "set apart." To be sanctified is to be set apart from sin. At conversion, all believers are disengaged from sin's bondage, released from sin's captivity—set apart unto God, or sanctified. Yet the process of separation from sin is only begun at that moment. As we grow in Christ, we become more separated from sin and more consecrated to God. Thus the sanctification that occurs at conversion only initiates a lifelong process whereby we are set apart more and more from sin and brought more and more into conformity with Christ—separated from sin, and separated unto God.

A CHANGE OF NATURE

"If anyone is in Christ, he is a new creation; old things have passed away; behold, all things have become new" (2 Corinthians 5:17).

When you receive Jesus Christ, are born again, and enter into God's kingdom, you become a totally different individual. The change that occurs when you're saved is more dramatic than the change that will occur when you die because then you already have a new nature and are a citizen of God's kingdom.

Death simply ushers you into God's presence. In his epistles, the apostle Paul said that when God transformed us, He gave us a new will, mind, heart, power, knowledge, wisdom, life, inheritance, relationship, righteousness, love, desire, and citizenship. He called it "newness of life" (Romans 6:4).

Some teach that when a person becomes a Christian, God gives him something new in addition to his old sin nature. But according to the Word of God, we don't receive something new—we ourselves become new!

The New Nature

"Having been born again, not of corruptible seed but incorruptible, through the word of God which lives and abides forever" (1 Peter 1:23).

When we become Christians we are not remodeled, nor are we added to—we are transformed.

Christians don't have two different natures; we have one new nature, the new nature in Christ. The old self dies and the new self lives; they do not coexist. Jesus Christ is righteous, holy, and sanctified, and we have that divine principle in us—what Peter called the "incorruptible" seed (1 Peter 1:23). Thus our new nature is righteous, holy, and sanctified because Christ lives in us through His Spirit (Colossians 1:27).

Ephesians 4:24 tells us to "put on the new man," a new behavior that's appropriate to our new nature. But to do so we have to eliminate the patterns and practices of our old life. That's why Paul tells us to "put to death your members which are on the earth: fornication, uncleanness, passion, evil desire, and covetousness" (Colossians 3:5).

CONFORMING TO CHRIST

"Do not love the world or the things in the world" (1 John 2:15).

As Christians, we are new creations and members of the church of Jesus Christ, and therefore unique. As a result, we should not live like people in the world. The world is proud; we are humble. The world is fragmented; we are united. The world is impotent; we are gifted. The world is hateful; we are full of love. The world doesn't know the truth; we do. If we don't walk any differently from the world, we won't accomplish Christ's goals. If we live like people in the world, we essentially are imitating the dead (Ephesians 2:1–5), and that doesn't make sense.

Christians are like a new race. We have a new spiritual, incorruptible seed, and we must live a lifestyle that corresponds to it. We are new creations who have been suited for an eternal existence. As a result, we can discard our old lifestyle and be conformed to the life of Christ.

Think Differently

"You should no longer walk as the rest of the Gentiles walk, in the futility of their mind" (Ephesians 4:17).

Salvation is—first and foremost—a change of mind. The apostle Paul wrote to believers, "You have not so learned Christ" (Ephesians 4:20). Christianity is cognitive before it is experiential. A person needs to consider the gospel, believe its historic facts and spiritual truths, and then receive Christ as Savior and Lord.

The first step in that process is repentance, which means that you think differently about sin, about God, about Christ, and about your life than you used to think. The Greek word for repentance means "to change one's mind." As it is used in the New Testament, it always refers to a change of purpose, specifically a turning from sin.

That change should result in a change of behavior, which also is based on the mind. Paul says that unregenerate people live "in the futility of their mind." Proverbs 23:7 says, "As he thinks in his heart, so is he." So when you think differently, you will act differently.

Live in Light

"You are the light of the world. A city that is set on a hill cannot be hidden" (Matthew 5:14).

The apostle Paul looked at the evil pagan world and concluded that its self-centered, useless thinking leads to darkened understanding and a hard heart. That, in turn, leads to insensitivity to sin and shameless behavior, which then leads to unblushing obscenity. And it's not really much different today. As believers we shouldn't even dabble in any of the evils characteristic of unbelievers. We are to be a light on a hill, separate from the evil around us. We are to be different. A city that's set on a hill can't be hidden. We must stand as salt and light. But if we're corrupted by the system, we become useless.

Our blessed Lord Jesus Christ purchased us at the cost of His own life. He gave us a new nature that is holy, undefiled, and sanctified forever. He simply asks us to live up to what He has given us by discarding our old lifestyle and taking on our new one.

Examine Yourself

"Do you not know that friendship with the world is enmity with God? Whoever therefore wants to be a friend of the world makes himself an enemy of God" (James 4:4).

Are you still hanging on to the lifestyle you followed before you became a Christian? If you didn't make a conscious effort to cut yourself off from this world when you came to Christ, you have reason to question whether your salvation was genuine.

First John 2:15 says, "Do not love the world or the things in the world. If anyone loves the world, the love of the Father is not in him." When you become a Christian, your desire should be to cut yourself off from the world. Certainly the world will continue to tempt you from time to time, but you're to forsake the devil's evil system.

To say that a person can come to Christ without making a break from the world is a lie. There must be a change of lifestyle! It's not an easy thing to do—Paul commanded us not to live as we did before we came to Christ (Ephesians 4:17). But we can live this life because we have a new nature.

THE IMPORTANCE OF REPENTANCE

No one can come to Jesus Christ unless he repents. Jesus began His ministry proclaiming the need for repentance (Matthew 4:17), and both Peter and Paul continued to proclaim it. Repentance is a conscious choice to turn from the world, sin, and evil.

It Is Crucial!

If you came to Jesus Christ thinking all you had to do was believe but didn't have to confess your sin or be willing to cut yourself off from the evil of this world, you have missed the point of salvation. Many people's lives haven't changed at all since they supposedly believed in Christ. For example, some acted immorally and still act immorally. Some committed adultery and continue to commit adultery. And some committed fornication and continue to commit fornication. Yet according to 1 Corinthians 6:9–10, fornicators and adulterers will not inherit the kingdom of God. If you are really saved, you will make a conscious attempt to break away from the things of the world.

A CHRIST-CENTERED LIFE

As Christians, we are no longer controlled by a self-centered mind; we learn from Christ. Christ thinks for us, acts through us, loves through us, feels through us, and serves through us. The lives we live are not ours but are Christ living in us (Galatians 2:20).

Philippians 2:5 says, "Let this mind be in you which was also in Christ Jesus." An unsaved person walks in the vanity of his own mind, but a saved person walks according to the mind of Christ.

God has a plan for the universe, and as long as Christ is working in us, He's working out a part of that plan through us. Paul noted that He "is able to do exceedingly abundantly above all that we ask or think, according to the power that works in us" (Ephesians 3:20).

Every day should be a fantastic adventure for us because we're in the middle of God's unfolding plan for the ages.

A RENEWED MIND

When you become a Christian, God gives you a new mind (see Ephesians 4:23)—but you must fill it with new thoughts. A baby is born with a fresh, new mind, and then impressions are made in the baby's mind that determine the course of his or her life. The same thing is true of a Christian. When you enter into God's kingdom, you're given a fresh, new mind. You then need to build the right thoughts into your new mind.

That's why Philippians 4:8 says, "Whatever things are true, whatever things are noble, whatever things are just, whatever things are pure, whatever things are lovely, whatever things are of good report, if there is any virtue and if there is anything praiseworthy—meditate on these things." We have a renewed mind, not a reprobate mind.

Instead of having a reprobate, vile, lascivious, greedy, unclean mind, we have a mind filled with righteousness and holiness. And that should naturally characterize the way we live.

A NEW ATTITUDE

"Put on the new man which was created according to God, in true righteousness and holiness" (Ephesians 4:24).

When you came to Christ, you acknowledged that you were a sinner and chose to forsake your sin and the evil things of this world. But Satan will dangle the world and its sin in front of you to tempt you to return to it. Paul warned us not to return to it but to put it off and instead, put on righteousness and true holiness.

That's not something you do once; it's something you do every day. One way you do so is described in 2 Timothy 3:16, which says, "All Scripture is given by inspiration of God, and is profitable for doctrine, for reproof, for correction, for instruction in righteousness."

If you want to live correctly, expose yourself to the Word of God. It will help you deal with the traces of the world still present in your life.

FOCUS ON THE TRUTH

A Christian should never tell any type of lie. The most familiar kind of lie is saying something that isn't true. But there are other kinds, such as exaggeration. I once heard the story of a certain Christian man who shared a powerful testimony, but one day he stopped reciting it. When asked why, he said that through the years he had embellished it so much he had forgotten what was true and what he'd made up.

Cheating in school, in business, at work, and on your taxes is a form of lying. So is the betrayal of a confidence, flattery, making excuses, and remaining silent when the truth should be spoken. There's no place for lying in the Christian life. We are to tell the truth.

The Importance of Truth

"Therefore, putting away lying, 'Let each one of you speak truth with his neighbor,' for we are members of one another" (Ephesians 4:25).

Why is it so important to tell the truth? Because we are members one of another. When we don't speak the truth with each other, we harm our fellowship. For example, what would happen if your brain told you that cold was hot and hot was cold? When you took a shower, you'd either freeze to death or scald yourself! If your eye decided to send false signals to your brain, a dangerous curve in the highway might appear straight and you would crash. You depend on the honesty of your nervous system and of every organ in your body.

The body of Christ can't function with any less than that. We cannot shade the truth with others and expect the church to function properly. How can we minister to each other, bear each other's burdens, care for each other, love each other, build up each other, teach each other, and pray for each other if we do not know what is going on in each others' lives? So be honest, "speaking the truth in love" (Ephesians 4:15).

RIGHTEOUS ANGER

You might be surprised to hear that there is such a thing as righteous anger—that is, being angry over what grieves God and hinders His causes.

But we are not to be so angry that it results in sin (Ephesians 4:26). Don't be angry for your own causes. Don't get angry when people offend you. And don't let your anger degenerate into personal resentment, bitterness, sullenness, or moodiness. That is forbidden. The only justifiable anger defends the great, glorious, and holy nature of our God.

Anger that is selfish, passionate, undisciplined, and uncontrolled is sinful, useless, and hurtful. It must be banished from the Christian life. But the disciplined anger that seeks the righteousness of God is pure, selfless, and dynamic. We ought to be angry about the sin in the world and in the church. But we can't let that anger degenerate into sin.

HARD WORK

Paul wrote, "Let him who stole steal no longer, but rather let him labor, working with his hands what is good, that he may have something to give him who has need" (Ephesians 4:28).

Theft is a common problem in our world. Shoplifting has become such a problem that a significant percentage of the price of commercial items covers the amount lost from stolen goods. Whether grand theft or petty theft, robbing from the store, or stealing money from a rich man or a family member, it is all stealing.

Christians are to "labor," which refers to hard, manual work. Hard work is honorable. As Christians we should work hard so that we will have enough to give to those in need, not so that we will have more of what we don't need. The worldly approach to wealth is to hoard what we acquire. But the New Testament principle is to work hard so we might do good and give to those who have needs.

SPEECH

Rotten fruit smells terrible and is worthless. You don't want to get near it, let alone eat it. The same thing is true of rotten language. Whether it is off-color jokes, profanity, dirty stories, or crude speech, in no way should it characterize a Christian.

Psalm 141:3 tells us how to eliminate such speech: "Set a guard, O LORD, over my mouth; keep watch over the door of my lips." If Jesus Christ is the door-keeper of your lips, He will be the one to determine what comes out of them.

Edifying Words

If you allow Christ to keep watch over your lips, whatever you say should build up others. You should encourage and strengthen others spiritually (see Ephesians 4:29).

Is that what happens when you talk with people? Do they go away built up in Jesus Christ? Mothers, when you are with your children throughout the day, do your words build them up? Fathers, when you take your children out for the day, are your conversations with them edifying and encouraging?

This verse also indicates that we should give others "necessary" edification, meaning that our words fit the need. When I was growing up, whenever I would say to my mom, "Do you know what

So-and-so did?" she would respond, "Is that necessary to know?" Often what I wanted to say was interesting, but it certainly wasn't necessary.

Finally, our speech should "impart grace to the hearers." Do your words bless those who hear them? Is there graciousness in what you say? You can be sure that if you allow the Lord to set a watch over your tongue and let His Word dwell in you, then your words will be His gracious words.

OUR GRACIOUS SPIRIT

"Do not grieve the Holy Spirit of God, by whom you were sealed for the day of redemption" (Ephesians 4:30).

The Holy Spirit grieves (is saddened) when believers don't exchange their old lifestyle for the new one. He is grieved when believers lie and obscure the truth, when they're angry and unforgiving, when they steal and refuse to share, and when they speak corruptly and lack a spirit of graciousness.

When you were saved, the Spirit of God put a seal on you, declaring that you belong to God forever. Since He has been gracious enough to give you eternal salvation, seal you forever, and keep your salvation secure until the day of redemption, how could you willfully grieve Him? He has done so much for you that, as a token of gratitude, you should not grieve Him.

EVIDENCE OF BELIEF

The apostle John made love for God the true mark of the believer. He quoted Jesus, saying, "If anyone loves Me, he will keep My word; and My Father will love him, and We will come to him and make Our home with him. He who does not love Me does not keep My words; and the word which you hear is not Mine but the Father's who sent Me" (John 14:23–24). In his first epistle, John wrote, "But whoever keeps His word, truly the love of God is perfected in him. By this we know that we are in Him" (1 John 2:5; see also 3:17; 4:12–13). You'll notice how these verses connect love for God with keeping His Word.

Where does this ability to love come from? John explained, "He who does not love does not know God, for God is love" (1 John 4:8). The source of our love is its very object, the One who is the essence of love, whether expressed in consolation or in wrath and judgment.

Jesus enabled us to receive His love because He died for our sin of hating God. Now He enables us to love God, because it is through Him that "the love of God has been poured out in our hearts by the Holy Spirit who was given to us" (Romans 5:5). First John 4:19 confirms this wonderful truth: "We love Him because He first loved us."

God's Standard

The Christian life could be summed up in this one statement: be mimics, or imitators, of God. Jesus said, "Therefore you shall be perfect, just as your Father in heaven is perfect" (Matthew 5:48). The apostle Peter reiterated that high standard when he said, "But as He who called you is holy, you also be holy in all your conduct, because it is written, 'Be holy, for I am holy'" (1 Peter 1:15–16).

The more you know God, the more you'll understand who He wants you to be, so the primary pursuit of any believer is to know God (Philippians 3:10). That can be achieved only when we study God's character as it is revealed in Scripture.

Be a Mimic

"Be imitators of God as dear children" (Ephesians 5:1).

Imitating God may be easy to discuss, but it is difficult to do. You cannot do it in your own strength. But Jesus gave us the starting point for imitating God in the Sermon on the Mount. We need to mourn over our sin with a broken and contrite spirit. When we are overwhelmed by our sinfulness, we will hunger and thirst for righteousness. So there is a paradox: we are to be like God, yet we must know we cannot be like Him on our own.

Once we are aware of the paradox, then we know there must be some other power to make imitating God a possibility. The apostle Paul prayed that God would strengthen us "with might through His Spirit in the inner man" (Ephesians 3:16). The Holy Spirit provides the strength "that you may be filled with all the fullness of God" (v. 19). We can be like God (in terms of His character), but we can't do it on our own—that is the Spirit's work.

Unconditional Love

The Bible doesn't refer to Christian love as an emotion but as an act of self-sacrifice. A person who truly loves someone else doesn't try to get anything out of that person. That's because godly love is never conditioned on a response—it is unconditional.

The world often defines love in terms of what it can get. But God loves even if He never gets anything in return. If that kind of love characterized our marriages, the divorce rate wouldn't be what it is today.

If those who claim they don't love their spouses anymore would commit themselves to loving them unconditionally, they just might find that they can recapture or rebuild their love. Our Lord Jesus Christ doesn't love us for what He can get out of us; He loves us in spite of the hurt we cause Him. Make unconditional love your goal, and be humble, obedient, and self-sacrificing.

The World's Search for Love

The people of the world want love very much. Loving, being loved, and making love are viewed as the ultimate high. Love is seen as the way to experience emotional extremes: you'll never be as happy nor as sad as when you're in love.

Today's music feeds that quest for love. Throughout much of it is the same underlying message: either the fantasy of a love sought or the despair of a love lost. People continue to chase that elusive dream. They base their concept of love on what it does for them. Songs, plays, films, books, and TV programs continually perpetuate the fantasy—the dream of a perfect love perfectly fulfilled.

The world's love is unforgiving, conditional, and self-centered. It focuses on desire, self-pleasure, and lust—the very opposite of God's perfect love. People search for love, but it's not true love; it is Satan's perversion.

Satan's Bill of Goods

"But fornication and all uncleanness or covetousness, let it not even be named among you, as is fitting for saints; neither filthiness, nor foolish talking, nor coarse jesting, which are not fitting, but rather giving of thanks" (Ephesians 5:3–4).

God's love and the love of His children is forgiving, unconditional, and self-sacrificing, but you can be sure Satan will pervert that. Worldly love is shallow, selfish, sensual, and sexual, and Satan has sold that definition of love to the world.

In contrast to the world's love, this verse concludes by indicating that we are to give thanks. Paul said, "In everything give thanks; for this is the will of God in Christ Jesus for you" (1 Thessalonians 5:18). When we are thankful for everything, we step outside ourselves, because thanksgiving is directed toward God.

Instead of taking from people, love them in a way that communicates thankfulness. Remember, God's love is unselfish and thankful, but the world's love is selfish and thankless.

AVOID THE CAVE

We are to walk in the light. When a Christian sins and engages in the deeds of darkness, it's as if he has had a relapse (see John 12:35).

Imagine yourself lost in a cave. As you attempt to find your way out, you only proceed deeper and deeper into the network of tunnels. Soon you're in the belly of the earth. You're scared. Your heart is pounding. Your eyes are wide open, but all you can see is an oppressive blackness. You grope for hours, and the hours become a day, and then another day. All hope seems lost.

Suddenly, off in the distance, there is a pinpoint of light. You move toward it, groping lest you fall into a deeper pit. Finally the light begins to widen and you find yourself at an opening in the cave! With your remaining strength you charge out into the daylight.

You then know a freedom like nothing you had ever conceived was possible. However, not long after your escape you decide there were several things you enjoyed in the cave. So you go back in. How foolish! Yet that is essentially what a Christian does when he follows after deeds of darkness.

The Proof's in the Light

The joy of a Christian is to be a living example of God's truth—to be a living verification of what is pleasing to Him.

When I was in Damascus, I discovered that the shops don't have windows. If you want to buy something, you have to take it out into the street and hold it up to the light to detect any flaws. Similarly, the only way to evaluate our lives is to expose every action, decision, and motive to the light of Christ and His Word.

When I go to the airport and put my suitcase through the scanner, I never worry about what the guard might see. I don't have anything to hide. I don't carry any guns or bombs. That's the way we ought to be as Christians. We shouldn't mind having the light reveal what we are, because it should only verify the truthfulness of our identity. We ought to be willing to expose our lives to light so that it will prove that we are light.

Exposing Sin

Rather than doing what people in the world do, we ought to be exposing their evil. You could call us the spiritual CIA: our job is to expose the crimes of darkness. Our tool is the Word of God: "All Scripture is inspired by God and profitable for teaching, for *reproof,* for correction, for training in righteousness" (2 Timothy 3:16 NASB, emphasis added). Our life and our words should expose evil.

Sometimes just the way you live can expose the evil in people's lives. Have you ever walked up to people who know you're a Christian and who happen to be in the middle of a filthy conversation? Does it suddenly turn clean? When some unbelievers I happened to be playing golf with found out I was a pastor, their words and attitudes changed immediately.

We also are commissioned by God to verbally expose the evil of the world. We must diagnose it, confront it, and then offer the solution. Sin is a cancer that must be removed. You aren't helping anyone by ignoring it. People need to be convicted about their sin before they will ever see their need for a Savior.

WAKE UP!

"Therefore He says: 'Awake, you who sleep, arise from the dead, and Christ will give you light'" (Ephesians 5:14).

This verse quotes what the prophet Isaiah said in Isaiah 60:1: "Arise, shine; for your light has come! And the glory of the LORD is risen upon you." That verse looked forward to the Messiah, and Paul's interpretation looks back to what Christ has done.

Many Bible commentators believe that Ephesians 5:14 is a line from an Easter hymn sung by the early church. They see it as an invitation—a gospel presentation. The sinner is the one who sleeps, and the invitation is to awake and arise. The Savior is Christ, who will give light.

Like Rip Van Winkle, men and women are sleeping through an age—an age of grace. When they wake up it will be too late. So Paul encourages them, as should we, to awake and arise from the dead.

CHAPTER 5

CONFESSION AND RESTORATION

CONFESSION OF SIN

In the parable of the prodigal son, the father's response illustrates God's love toward a penitent sinner and the power of confession. Even while the profligate boy is still a long way off, the father sees him (which means the father must have been looking for his wayward son). He "ran and embraced him, and kissed him" (Luke 15:20 NASB). The verb tense indicates that he kissed him over and over. Here is tender mercy. Here is forgiveness. Here is compassion. Here is a father treating the son as if there were no past, as if his sins had been buried in the depths of the deepest sea, removed as far as the east is from the west, and forgotten. Here is unrestrained affection, unconditional love.

The father's response is remarkable. There is no diffidence. There is no hesitation. There is no withholding of emotion, no subtle coolness. There is only sympathetic, eager, pure, unbridled love. The father loves his wayward child lavishly. He loves him profusely. He loves him grandly.

The son seems shocked by this. He begins the speech he had rehearsed: "Father, I have sinned against heaven and in your sight; I am no longer worthy to be called your son" (v. 21 NASB). It's almost as if he can't deal with his father's tender affection. He is consumed by his own sense of unworthiness. He is in the throes of profound humiliation. He is fully aware of the seriousness of his sin. After all, he had been reduced to eating with pigs. Now, being showered with a loving father's kisses must have only increased his sense of utter shame.

The father's grace was, if anything, even more humbling than the prodigal son's awareness of his own sin. The young man knew in his heart that he was completely undeserving. And so he confessed, "I am no longer worthy to be called your son."

But here we are concerned primarily with the father's response. Notice that he doesn't even respond to the son's hesitancy:

> But the father said to his slaves, "Quickly bring out the best robe and put it on him, and put a ring on his hand and sandals on his feet; and bring the fattened calf, kill it, and let us eat and be merry; for this son of mine was dead, and has come to life again; he was lost, and has been found." And they began to be merry. (vv. 22–24 NASB)

He pays no attention whatsoever to the penitent young man's confession of unworthiness. He just orders his servants to start the celebration. He showers the prodigal son with favors. He gives him the best robe. He puts a ring on his hand. He gets sandals for his feet. And he kills the fatted calf.

There's much more that could be said about this parable, of course. There are rich spiritual lessons to be drawn from the nature of the prodigal's repentance, the response of the elder brother, and many other aspects of the parable. But the point that interests us here is how Jesus pictured the love of God toward a penitent sinner.

God's love is like the love of this father. It is not minimal; it is unreserved. It is unrestrained. It is extravagant. It is not bestowed in moderation. There is no holding back—just pure love undiluted, without any resentment or disaffection. The father receives the wayward boy as a privileged son, not as a lowly servant.

Above all, the love of the father was an unconditional love. It was undiminished by the rebellion of the son. Despite all that this boy had done to deserve his father's wrath, the father responded with unrestrained love. Though the young man may not have realized it while he was languishing in the far country, he could not be estranged from so loving a father. Even his great sins could not ultimately separate him from his father's love.

Our Father wants us to return and to confess— He waits with open arms.

GENUINE REPENTANCE

Repentance is no more a meritorious work than its counterpart, faith. It is an *inward* response. Genuine repentance pleads with the Lord to forgive and deliver from the burden of sin and the fear of judgment and hell. It is the attitude of the publican who, fearful of even looking toward heaven, smote his breast and cried, "God, be merciful to me, the sinner!" (Luke 18:13 NASB). Repentance is not merely behavior reform. But because true repentance involves a change of heart and purpose, it inevitably *results* in a change of behavior.

Like faith, repentance has intellectual, emotional, and volitional ramifications. Louis Berkhof describes the *intellectual* element of repentance as "a change of view, a recognition of sin as involving personal guilt, defilement, and helplessness." The *emotional* element is "a change of feeling, manifesting itself in sorrow for sin committed against a holy God." The *volitional* element is "a change of purpose, an inward turning away from sin, and a disposition to seek pardon and cleansing."[1] Each of those three elements is deficient apart from the others. Repentance is a response of the total person; therefore some speak of it as total surrender.

CHAPTER 6

ULTIMATE
DESTINATION

Is it possible to have full assurance of one's salvation? Can Christians rest in the firm and settled confidence that they are redeemed and bound for eternal heaven?

Scripture categorically answers yes. Resting in the knowledge that God is sovereign and Lord of our lives should give us confidence, security, and assurance. Not only does the Bible teach that assurance is *possible* for Christians in this life, but the apostle Peter also gave this command: "[Be] diligent to make certain about His calling and choosing you" (2 Peter 1:10 NASB). Assurance is not only a privilege; it is the birthright and sacred trust of every true child of God. We are commanded to *cultivate* assurance, not take it for granted.

True assurance is a taste of heaven on earth. Fanny Crosby expressed that truth in a well-known hymn: "Blessed assurance, Jesus is Mine! O what a foretaste of glory divine!" Puritan Thomas Brooks observed the same reality and entitled his book on assurance *Heaven on Earth*. To possess genuine assurance is to experience a bit of divine bliss this side of heaven. The greater our sense of assurance, the more we can savor that glory in this earthly life.

In contemporary Christianity assurance is too often either ignored, or claimed by people who have no right to it. Too many people believe they are saved merely because someone told them so. They do not examine themselves; they do not test their assurance by God's Word; they are taught that doubts about their salvation can only be detrimental to spiritual health and growth. Yet multitudes of these people give no evidence of any spiritual health or growth whatsoever.

ASSURANCE IN THE REFORMATION

Assurance is an issue that was at the heart of the Protestant Reformation. The Roman Catholic Church denied—and denies to this day—that anyone on earth can have assurance of salvation. Because Catholic theology sees salvation as a joint effort between God and the sinner, the outcome must be in doubt right up to the end. If a person fails spiritually before salvation is complete, that person forfeits eternal life. Since no one can know with certainty whether he or she will have the strength to endure to the end, no one can really be certain of heaven.[1]

The Reformers, by contrast, taught that believers can and should be fully assured of their salvation. The early Reformers went so far as to define faith in a way that included assurance. Calvin's definition of faith is often quoted: "It is a firm and sure knowledge of the divine favour toward us, founded on the truth of a free promise in Christ, and revealed to our minds, and sealed on our hearts, by the Holy Spirit."[2] Calvin emphasized faith as *knowledge,* in contrast to the Catholic Scholastics' idea that faith is a naïve trust antithetical to knowledge. He thus built assurance into his definition of faith. In other words, Calvin taught that *assurance is of the essence of faith.* That means the moment someone trusts Christ for salvation, that person will have *some* sense of assurance. Hebrews 11:1 says, "Faith is the assurance of things hoped for, the conviction of things not seen" (NASB). Thus it seems clear from Scripture that a measure of assurance *is* inherent in believing.

Often, however, the assurance of faith is darkened by doubt. Calvin also recognized that self-doubt can coexist with true belief. He wrote, "When we say that faith must be certain and secure, we certainly speak not of an assurance which is never affected by doubt, nor a security which anxiety never assails, we rather maintain that believers have a perpetual struggle with their own distrust, and are thus far from thinking that their consciences possess a placid quiet, uninterrupted by perturbation [distress]."[3]

Scripture is clearly on Calvin's side here. Some assurance belongs to the essence of faith, but believing does not necessarily bring *full* assurance. "I do believe; help my unbelief" (Mark 9:24 NASB) is a sincere expression of every new believer's heart. Even the apostles pleaded with Jesus, "Increase our faith" (Luke 17:5).

Later Reformed theologians, recognizing that genuine Christians often lack assurance, denied that *any* assurance is implicit in believing. On this issue they were in disagreement with Calvin. Calvin, arguing against Rome, was eager to emphasize the possibility of immediate assurance. The later Reformers, battling antinomian tendencies in their movement, wanted to emphasize the importance of practical evidence in the lives of believers.

The Westminster Confession of Faith, drawn up in 1646, distinguishes faith from assurance. The Confession includes this:

> This infallible assurance *doth not so belong to the essence of faith, but that a true believer may wait long, and conflict with many difficulties before he be partaker of it*: yet, being enabled by the Spirit to know the things which are freely given him of God, he may, without extraordinary revelation, in the right use of ordinary means, attain thereunto. And therefore it is the duty of every one to give all diligence to make his calling and election sure. (Chapter 18 Section III, emphasis added)

In other words, the Confession taught that assurance is something distinct from faith. A person can thus become a genuine believer, yet remain unsure of salvation. To the Westminster divines, assurance was possible—even highly desirable—but not automatic. They believed some Christians need to "wait long" and wrestle with God before He grants them assurance. Most of the Puritans (seventeenth-century English Reformers) shared this view on assurance.

So on the one hand, Calvin tended to make the grounds for assurance wholly *objective*, urging believers to look to the promises of Scripture to gain a sense of personal assurance. On the other hand, the Puritans tended to emphasize *subjective* means of establishing assurance, counseling people to examine their lives and behavior for evidences of their election.[4]

In fact, some of the Puritans carried their teaching on assurance to implausible extremes. They tended to become mystical on the issue, implying that assurance was something God grants supernaturally in His time and in special measures for select saints—almost like a heavenly vision one could be zapped with, or an added work of grace. Most of the Puritans taught that believers could not expect assurance until long after conversion, and only after a life of extended faithfulness.[5] They tended to make assurance dependent on the believer's ability to live at an almost unattainable level of personal holiness. I have profited greatly from reading their works, but I often wonder how many of them were able to live up to their own standards.

As we might expect, the Puritans' demanding preaching led to a widespread *lack* of assurance among their flocks. Christians became obsessed with whether they were truly elect, and many lapsed into morbid introspection and utter despair. That explains why so much of the Puritan literature is written for people struggling with the question of assurance.

By contrast, today assurance is rarely made an issue. Few professing Christians seem to lack assurance because evangelistic preaching is usually devoid of any call to holy living. Evangelists and counselors normally seek to dispel doubts about salvation by pronouncing them groundless, or by teaching converts to view all doubt as an attack by the enemy. Preachers are so fearful of shattering anyone's confidence that they seem to forget *false* assurance is a more serious problem than *no* assurance (Matthew 7:21–23). Surely there is a middle ground. Scripture encourages *true believers* with the promise of full assurance, while making *false professors* uncomfortable by seeking to destroy their false sense of security. A true believer's sense of assurance should not rise and fall with the emotions; assurance is meant to be an anchor even in the midst of life's difficulties. But a false professor has no right to assurance. Aren't those the twin emphases our preaching should reflect? Can we recover a biblical understanding of assurance?

We must. This is where the lordship debate touches almost every Christian at the most practical level. If we confuse the issue of assurance, we will have multitudes, on the one hand, whose spiritual lives are crippled by doubt, and multitudes, on the other, who expect to be ushered into heaven but will one day be devastated to hear the Lord say, "I never knew you; depart from Me" (Matthew 7:23).

IS ASSURANCE OBJECTIVE OR SUBJECTIVE?

The difference between Calvin and the Puritans raises a question: Should Christians seek assurance through clinging only to the *objective* promises of Scripture, or through *subjective* self-examination? If we opt for the objective promises only, those who profess faith in Christ while denying Him by their deeds (Titus 1:16) can claim an assurance they have no entitlement to. But if we say assurance is available only through subjective self-examination, we render full assurance practically impossible and make assurance a wholly mystical affair.

Those who argue for a subjective approach will point out that Scripture clearly calls for self-examination. We are commanded to examine ourselves regularly—at least as often as we participate in the Lord's Supper (1 Corinthians 11:28). Paul also issued this challenge to the church at Corinth: "Test yourselves to see if you are in the faith; examine yourselves! Or do you not recognize this about yourselves, that Jesus Christ is in you—unless indeed you fail the test?" (2 Corinthians 13:5 NASB). Clearly Paul was dealing here with the matter of assurance. The Corinthians were to test themselves *to see if they were "in the faith."* But what kind of self-examination was Paul calling for? What was the "test" the Corinthians needed to pass? Was the apostle counseling them to look within themselves and anchor their assurance on their own goodness? Was he challenging them to think back and remember some moment of faith on which they could fix their hopes? Or was he suggesting that they should look to their works and place confidence in their spiritual accomplishments?

None of those suggestions answers the matter adequately. Works alone can no more guarantee genuine assurance than they can be the basis for eternal salvation. After all, external works can be performed even by non-Christians. On the other hand, as we have seen, even the most spiritual Christians discover sin when they look within. So no one's works measure up to God's standard of perfection. Those who only look within themselves to establish their assurance merely set themselves up for a life of frustration. Settled assurance cannot be found in any amount of works. If we must base our assurance solely on something in ourselves or our experience, our confidence will be resting on an inadequate foundation.[6] That approach to assurance is *too subjective.*

But the promises of God are sufficient for assurance. While one's works can have a confirmatory value, they are not essential for assurance. Any believer can have 100 percent certainty of his salvation if he but looks to the promises in God's Word to the believer.

One can have firm assurance of salvation and yet walk in sin. Sin, while a grievous thing, does not necessarily weaken assurance. Only if sin results in a person taking his eyes off God's promises can sin weaken assurance.[7]

Some argue that, as long as a person clings to the *objective promises* of God's Word, no amount of sin can trouble that person's assurance. Someone who chooses to "walk in sin" can do so with full assurance of faith.[8]

But that extreme cannot be supported practically *or* biblically. Hebrews 10:22 specifically says that to possess "full assurance of faith" we must have "our hearts sprinkled clean from an evil conscience." Second Peter 1:5–10 lists several spiritual virtues that are essential to salvation: faith, moral excellence, knowledge, self-control, perseverance, godliness, brotherly kindness, and love. The person "who lacks these qualities is blind or short-sighted, *having forgotten his purification from his former sins*" (v. 9 NASB, emphasis added). Those who "walk in sin" may be convinced in their *minds* that their salvation is secure, but unless their heart and conscience are utterly seared, they will have to admit that sin ruins their assurance. This approach to assurance is *too objective*.

WHAT ARE BIBLICAL GROUNDS FOR ASSURANCE?

The Bible suggests that a well-grounded assurance has both objective and subjective support.[9] The objective ground is *the finished work of Christ on our behalf,* including the promises of Scripture, which have their yea and amen in Him (2 Corinthians 1:20). The subjective ground is *the ongoing work of the Holy Spirit in our lives*, including His convicting and sanctifying ministries. Romans 15:4 mentions both aspects of assurance: "Whatever was written in earlier times was written for our instruction, so that through *perseverance* [subjective] *and the encouragement of the Scriptures* [objective] we might have hope" (NASB, emphasis added).

Both the objective and subjective grounds for our assurance are applied to us by the Holy Spirit, who "bears witness with our spirit that we are children of God" (Romans 8:16).

The objective basis for our assurance includes the truth of justification by faith, the promise that Christ will never leave us or forsake us (Hebrews 13:5), the guarantee of our security in Christ (Romans 8:38–39), and all the objective truths of God's Word on which our faith is founded. The objective question asks, "Do you believe?" If you *truly* believe, you can be sure you are saved (John 3:16; Acts 16:31).

The subjective question asks, "Is your faith real?" That is the question Paul was asking in 2 Corinthians 13:5. What *kind* of self-examination was Paul calling for in that verse? We know that he was not suggesting Christians may find assurance in themselves or in their works. What, then, is the test we must pass?

Paul had hinted at the answer several chapters earlier in the same epistle. In 2 Corinthians 3:18 he wrote, "We all, with unveiled face, beholding as in a mirror the glory of the Lord, are being transformed into the same image from glory to glory, just as from the Lord, the Spirit" (NASB). As true Christians look into the mirror of God's Word (James 1:23), they should see the glory of the Lord reflected back. To be sure, it is a dim reflection. "Now we see in a mirror dimly, but then face to face; now I know in part, but then I will know fully just as I also have been fully known" (1 Corinthians 13:12 NASB). But it is that dim reflection of *His* glory—not anything inherent in us—that is the subjective basis for our assurance.

Even Calvin recognized a subjective ground for assurance, though it was not a major emphasis in his teaching. While emphasizing that all works are non-meritorious, Calvin said believers' good works are "divine gifts in which [believers] recognize [God's] goodness and signs of calling, in which they discern their election."[10] They are *God's* work in us, not our own accomplishments. In this same context Calvin quotes a prayer of Augustine: "'I commend not the works of my hands, for I fear that when thou examinest them thou wilt find more faults than merits. This only I say, this ask, this desire, Despise not the works of thy hands. See in me thy work, not mine. If thou seest mine, thou condemnest; if thou seest thine own, thou crownest. Whatever good works I have are of thee' (Augst. In Ps. Cxxxvii)."[11]

God's glory—albeit a dim reflection of that glory—is what we will see in the mirror if we are true believers. This is the test Paul laid before the Corinthians: Can you see Christ's glory reflected in you—even dimly? "Test yourselves to see if you are in the faith; examine yourselves! Or *do you not recognize this about yourselves, that Jesus Christ is in you*—unless indeed you fail the test?" (2 Corinthians 13:5 NASB, emphasis added). The image of Christ in us thus provides the subjective ground of our assurance. In other words, Christ in you is the hope of glory (Colossians 1:27).

IN ORDER THAT YOU MAY KNOW

The New Testament Epistles are filled with enough material on assurance to fill volumes of commentary. It is not possible in a book of this nature to give a full overview of the New Testament doctrine of assurance. Even the little epistle of 1 John, written to deal with precisely the issue of assurance, is so rich with material that we cannot do full justice to it in these few pages. But I do want to underscore some of the highlights of this treasured epistle and its clear teaching on this subject. Surely no other passage of Scripture confronts no-lordship theology with more force than this brief but potent letter.

John's purpose statement is explicit in 1 John 5:13: "These things I have written to you who believe in the name of the Son of God, *so that you may know that you have eternal life*" (NASB, emphasis added). There the apostle spelled out his intention. He was not trying to make believers *doubt*; he wanted them to have full assurance. What he had to say will not shake genuine believers; though it should certainly alarm those with a false sense of assurance.

Note that the apostle presupposes faith in Christ as the bedrock of all assurance: "I have written to you who believe..." There is no place for self-examination outside of faith in Christ. So everything John says about assurance is predicated on faith in Christ and the promises of Scripture.[12]

Throughout this epistle the apostle John maintained a careful balance between the objective and subjective grounds of assurance. The objective evidence constitutes a *doctrinal* test. The subjective evidence is not a works test but a *moral* test. John moved in and out between the two kinds of tests. Here are the proofs he said will be evident in every genuine believer.

True Believers Walk in the Light

"If we say that we have fellowship with Him and yet walk in the darkness, we lie and do not practice the truth; but if we walk in the Light as He Himself is in the Light, we have fellowship with one another, and the blood of Jesus His Son cleanses us from all sin" (1 John 1:6–7 NASB). Throughout Scripture, light is used as a metaphor for truth—both intellectual and moral truth.

Psalm 119:105 says, "Your word is a lamp to my feet and a light to my path." Verse 130 adds, "The unfolding of Your words gives light; it gives understanding to the simple" (NASB). Proverbs 6:23 says, "For the commandment is a lamp, and the teaching is light" (NASB). Those verses all speak of truth as something that may be *known* and *obeyed*. It is both doctrinal and moral. The light of all truth is embodied in Christ, who said, "I am the Light of the world; he who follows Me will not walk in the darkness, but will have the Light of life" (John 8:12 NASB).

Walking in darkness is the antithesis of following Christ. All unsaved people walk in darkness; Christians have been delivered into the light: "You were formerly darkness, but now you are Light in the Lord; walk as children of Light" (Ephesians 5:8 NASB). "You, brethren, are not in darkness" (1 Thessalonians 5:4). To "walk in the light" means to live in the realm of truth. So all true believers are walking in the light—even when we sin. When we sin, "The blood of Jesus . . . cleanses us" (1 John 1:7). The verb tense there indicates that Christ's blood *continually* cleanses us. When we sin, we are already being cleansed, so that no darkness ever clouds the light in which we dwell (1 Peter 2:9). "Walk[ing] in the light" describes both positional and practical reality for the believer. To trust Jesus Christ is to walk in the light. To walk in the light is to heed the light and live accordingly. So in this first test the apostle points us to both the *objective* and *subjective* grounds of assurance. To determine if we walk in the light we must answer the objective question, "Do I believe?" as well as the subjective question, "Is my faith real?"

True Believers Confess Their Sin

"If we say that we have no sin, we are deceiving ourselves and the truth is not in us. If we confess our sins, He is faithful and righteous to forgive us our sins and to cleanse us from all unrighteousness. If we say that we have not sinned, we make Him a liar and His word is not in us. My little children, I am writing these things to you so that you may not sin. And if anyone sins, we have an Advocate with the Father, Jesus Christ the righteous" (1 John 1:8–2:1 NASB).

The word for confess (Gk., *homologeoη*) means "to say the same thing." To "confess our sins" means to agree with God about them. This is a characteristic of all true Christians. They agree with God about their sin. That means they hate their sin; they don't love it. They acknowledge that they are sinful, and yet they know they are forgiven and that they "have an Advocate with the Father" (1 John 2:1).

Here it seems the apostle is suggesting an *objective* test of assurance: "Do you believe?" Specifically, "Do you agree with what God has said about your sin?"

True assurance of salvation always goes hand in hand with an awareness of our own sinfulness. In fact, the more certain we are of salvation, the deeper our awareness of our sin becomes. John Owen wrote, "A man, then, may have a deep sense of sin all his days, walk under the sense of it continually, abhor himself for his ingratitude, unbelief, and rebellion against God, without any impeachment of his assurance."[13]

That may sound paradoxical, but it is the very thing that keeps Christians from falling into utter despair. We *know* we are sinners. We agree with God about that. We're not surprised to discover sin in our lives, but nevertheless we hate it. We know we are forgiven and cleansed and that Christ is our Advocate. Far from using that knowledge to justify our sin, however, we see it as a motivation to mortify sin all the more: "I am writing these things to you so *that you may not sin*" (1 John 2:1 NASB, emphasis added).

True Believers Keep His Commandments

"By this we know that we have come to know Him, if we keep His commandments. The one who says, 'I have come to know Him,' and does not keep His commandments, is a liar, and the truth is not in him" (1 John 2:3–4 NASB). "By this we know that we love the children of God, when we love God and observe His commandments. For this is the love of God, that we keep His commandments; and His commandments are not burdensome" (5:2–3 NASB).

Here the apostle focuses on the *subjective* ground for assurance. He is prodding us to ask the question, "Is my faith real?" Here's how we can be sure if we have come to know Him: we keep His commandments. This is a test of obedience. The Greek word translated "keep" in 1 John 2:3–4 conveys the idea of a watchful, observant obedience. It is not an obedience that is only the result of external pressure. It is the eager obedience of one who "keeps" the divine commandments as if they were something precious to guard.

In other words, this speaks of an obedience motivated by love. Verse 5 spells it out: "Whoever keeps His word, in him the love of God has truly been perfected. By this we know that we are in Him" (NASB).

Those who claim to know God yet despise His commandments are liars (v. 4). "They profess to know God, but by their deeds they deny Him, being detestable and disobedient and worthless for any good deed" (Titus 1:16 NASB).

True Believers Love the Brethren

This test and the previous one are closely related: "By this the children of God and the children of the devil are obvious: anyone who does not practice righteousness is not of God, nor the one who does not love his brother" (1 John 3:10 NASB). "The one who says he is in the light and yet hates his brother is in the darkness until now. The one who loves his brother abides in the light and there is no cause for stumbling in him. But the one who hates his brother is in the darkness and walks in the darkness, and does not know where he is going because the darkness has blinded his eyes" (2:9–11 NASB).

"We know that we have passed out of death into life, because we love the brethren. He who does not love abides in death. Everyone who hates his brother is a murderer; and you know that no murderer has eternal life abiding in him" (1 John 3:14–15 NASB). "By this we know that we love the children of God, when we love God and observe His commandments" (5:2 NASB). The reason these two tests are so closely related is that love perfectly fulfills the law. "He who loves his neighbor has fulfilled the law" (Romans 13:8 NASB). To love God and to love one's neighbor fulfills the whole moral law. Jesus said, "'You shall love the Lord your God with all your heart, and with all your soul, and with all your mind.' This is the great and foremost commandment. The second is like it, 'You shall love your neighbor as yourself.' On these two commandments depend the whole Law and the Prophets" (Matthew 22:37–40 NASB).

Love for fellow believers is a particularly important evidence of genuine faith. The point is not that love is intrinsic to us, or something that rises out of our own goodness. "Beloved, let us love one another, for *love is from God;* and everyone who loves is born of God and knows God" (1 John 4:7, emphasis added). The love that is evidence of true faith is *God's* love, which is being perfected in us: "If we love one another, God abides in us, and His love has been perfected in us" (4:12). Once again, it is that dim reflection of divine glory in us that provides the subjective ground of our assurance.

True Believers Affirm Sound Doctrine

Here we return to the objective ground: "You have an anointing from the Holy One, and you all know. I have not written to you because you do not know the truth, but because you do know it, and because no lie is of the truth. Who is the liar but the one who denies that Jesus is the Christ? This is the antichrist, the one who denies the Father and the Son" (1 John 2:20–22 NASB). "By this you know the Spirit of God: every spirit that confesses that Jesus Christ has come in the flesh is from God. . . . We are from God; he who knows God listens to us; he who is not from God does not listen to us. By this we know the spirit of truth and the spirit of error" (4:2, 6 NASB).

John was writing in opposition to an early form of the Gnostic heresy, which denied that Jesus Christ is fully God and fully man. He was saying that no one who truly is saved can fall into serious, Christ-denying error or heresy. Why? Because "you have an anointing from the Holy One . . . [and] the anointing which you received from Him abides in you, and you have no need for anyone to teach you; but as His anointing teaches you about all things, and is true and is not a lie, and just as it has taught you, you abide in

Him" (1 John 2:20, 27 NASB). Again, it is the divine work in us, not our own skill or achievements, that provide a sound basis for our assurance.

What about those who depart completely from sound doctrine? John answers that question explicitly: "They went out from us, but they were not really of us; for if they had been of us, they would have remained with us; but they went out, so that it would be shown that they all are not of us" (2:19 NASB).[14] Those who fall away and deny Christ only prove that their faith was never genuine to begin with.

True Believers Follow after Holiness

"If you know that He is righteous, you know that everyone also who practices righteousness is born of Him" (1 John 2:29 NASB). "And everyone who has this hope fixed on Him purifies himself, just as He is pure. Everyone who practices sin also practices lawlessness; and sin in lawlessness" (3:3–4 NASB). "No one who abides in Him sins; no one who sins has seen Him or knows Him. Little children, make sure no one deceives you . . . the one who practices sin is of the devil; for the devil has sinned from the beginning. The Son of God appeared for this purpose, to destroy the works of the devil. No one who is born of God practices sin, because His seed abides in him; and he cannot sin, because he is born of God" (3:6–9 NASB).

Those verses have tripped many people up. The key to their meaning is the definition of sin in 3:4: "Sin is lawlessness." The Greek word for lawlessness is *anomia*. It literally means "without law," and it describes those who live immoral, ungodly, unrighteous lives as a matter of continuous practice. They hate God's righteousness and perpetually live as if they were sovereign over God's law. This cannot be true of a genuine Christian. The apostle is clearly *not* making sinless perfection a test of salvation. After all, he began his epistle by saying, "If we say that we have no sin, we are deceiving ourselves and the truth is not in us" (1:8 NASB).

Nor is he making an issue about the frequency, duration, or magnitude of one's sins. All Christians sin. The issue John is raising here has to do with our attitude toward sin and righteousness, our heart's response when we *do* sin, and the overall direction of our walk.

The test is this: What is the object of your affections—sin or righteousness? If your chief love is sin, then you are "of the devil" (3:8, 10). If you love righteousness and practice righteousness, you are born of God (2:29). What is the direction of your affection? As John Owen aptly wrote, "Your state is not at all to be measured by the opposition that sin makes to you, but by the opposition you make to it."[15]

Those who cling to the *promise* of eternal life but care nothing for Christ's holiness have nothing to be assured of. Such people do not really believe. Either their professed "faith" in Christ is an utter sham, or they are simply deluded. If they did truly have their hope fixed on Christ, they would purify themselves, just as He is pure (3:3).

True Believers Have the Holy Spirit

This is the overarching test that sums up all the others: Does the Holy Spirit reside in you?[16] John wrote, "By this we know that we abide in Him and He in us, because He has given us of His spirit" (1 John 4:13 NASB). "The one who believes in the Son of God has the testimony in himself; the one who does not believe God has made Him a liar, because he has not believed in the testimony that God has given concerning His Son. And the testimony is this, that God has given us eternal life, and this life is in His Son" (5:10–11 NASB).

There is an echo of Pauline theology in these verses. Paul wrote, "The Spirit Himself bears witness with our spirit that we are children of God" (Romans 8:16). Scripture says, "On the evidence of two or three witnesses a matter shall be confirmed" (Deuteronomy 19:15 NASB; see also Matthew 18:16; 2 Corinthians 13:1). Romans 8:16 is saying that the Holy Spirit adds His testimony to the witness of our spirit, thereby confirming our assurance. This utterly dispels the notion that self-examination is tantamount to placing one's faith in one's own works. The evidence we seek through self-examination is nothing other than the fruit of the Spirit (Galatians 5:22–23), the proof that He resides within. It is on that testimony that our assurance is confirmed.

THE DANGER OF FALSE ASSURANCE

Before we move on, we must deal briefly with the issue of false assurance. Throughout 1 John the apostle attacks the false profession of those who have no right to assurance: "The one who says, 'I have come to know Him,' and does not keep His commandments, is a liar, and the truth is not in him" (2:4 NASB). "The one who hates his brother is in the darkness and walks in the darkness, and does not know where he is going because the darkness has blinded his eyes" (2:11 NASB). "Whoever denies the Son does not have the Father" (2:23). "The one who practices sin is of the devil" (3:8 NASB). "Everyone who hates his brother is a murderer; and you know that no murderer has eternal life abiding in him" (3:15 NASB). "The one who does not love does not know God" (4:8 NASB). "If someone says, 'I love God,' and hates his brother, he is a liar; for the one who does not love his brother whom he has seen, cannot love God whom he has not seen" (4:20 NASB).

Some teaching ignores the danger of false assurance. How? First of all, this view sees assurance and saving faith as virtually synonymous: "Simply put, [the gospel] message brings with it the assurance of salvation. When a person believes, that person has assurance of life eternal. How could it be otherwise? To doubt the guarantee of eternal life is to doubt the message itself. In short, if I do not believe that I am saved, I do not believe the offer that God has made to me. A person who has *never been sure* of eternal life has *never believed* the saving message of God."[17]

In effect, then, according to this view, a conviction of assurance in one's mind is the best evidence of salvation. "People know whether they believe something or not, and that is the real issue where God is concerned."[18] Obviously, there is no room in such a view for *false* assurance. Everyone who professes to trust Christ is encouraged to claim "100 percent assurance." Everyone who professes assurance is accepted as a genuine believer, even if that person's lifestyle opposes everything Christ stands for.

The conscience screams against such a doctrine! It promises an "assurance" that the heart will never affirm. It offers no real peace to the soul. Instead it makes assurance a wholly intellectual property. This doctrine is therefore forced to deny the subjective ground of assurance, because self-examination would immediately reveal the emptiness of every false professor's ungrounded hope. Laying half a foundation, it declares the building complete. The objective test is all they can endure. If the mind is convinced, there is no need to involve the conscience. That is the epitome of false assurance.

John Owen called false assurance a "notional apprehension of the pardon of the sin."[19] The effect of such assurance, Owen believed, is that "it rather secretly insinuates into the soul encouragements unto a continuance in [sin]. There are none in the world that deal worse with God than those who have an ungrounded persuasion of forgiveness. Carnal boldness, formality, and despising of God are the common issues of such a notion and persuasion."[20] "Where conscience accuses, [false assurance] must supply the defect."[21] Owen was not afraid to point out that those who turn the grace of our God into licentiousness are, after all, ungodly (Jude v. 4). "Let them profess what they will," Owen wrote, "they are ungodly men."[22]

No-lordship theology tells obstinately ungodly people that they can rest secure in the hope of heaven. That is not genuine assurance. Real assurance springs from faith that works, allowing us to look in the mirror and see beyond our sinful selves a reflection of *God's* glory that is dim but growing brighter in ever-increasing waves: "We all, with unveiled face, beholding as in a mirror the glory of the Lord, are being transformed into the same image

from glory to glory, just as from the Lord, the Spirit"
(2 Corinthians 3:18 NASB).[23]

SUMMARY

These articles of faith are fundamental to all evangelical teaching:

- Christ's death on the cross paid the full
  penalty for our sins and purchased eternal
  salvation. His atoning sacrifice enables God to
  justify sinners freely without compromising
  the perfection of divine righteousness
  (Romans 3:24–26). His resurrection from the
  dead declares His victory over sin and death
  (1 Corinthians 15:54–57).
- Salvation is by grace through faith in the Lord
  Jesus Christ alone—plus and minus nothing
  (Ephesians 2:8–9).
- Sinners cannot earn salvation or favor with God
  (Romans 8:8). God requires of those who are
  saved no preparatory works or prerequisite self-
  improvement (Romans 10:13; 1 Timothy 1:15).
- Eternal life is a gift of God (Romans 6:23).
- Believers are saved and fully justified before
  their faith ever produces a single righteous
  work (Ephesians 2:10).

- Christians can and do sin (1 John 1:8, 10). Even the strongest Christians wage a constant and intense struggle against sin in the flesh (Romans 7:15–24). Genuine believers sometimes commit heinous sins, as David did in 2 Samuel 11.

Alongside these truths, I believe Scripture teaches these:

- The gospel calls sinners to faith joined in oneness with repentance (Acts 2:38; 17:30; 20:21; 2 Peter 3:9). Repentance is turning away from sin (Acts 3:19; Luke 24:47). It is not a work but a divinely bestowed grace (Acts 11:18; 2 Timothy 2:25). Repentance is a change of heart, but genuine repentance will effect a change of behavior as well (Luke 3:8; Acts 26:18–20).
- Salvation is all God's work. Those who believe are saved utterly apart from any effort on their own (Titus 3:5). Even faith is a gift of God, not a work of man (Ephesians 2:1–5, 8). Real faith therefore cannot be defective or short-lived but endures forever (Philippians 1:6; Hebrews 11).
- The object of faith is Christ Himself, not only a creed or a promise (John 3:16). Faith therefore involves personal commitment to Christ

(2 Corinthians 5:15). In other words, all true believers follow Jesus (John 10:27–28).

- Real faith inevitably produces a changed life (2 Corinthians 5:17). Salvation includes a transformation of the inner person (Galatians 2:20). The nature of the Christian is different, new (Romans 6:6). The unbroken pattern of sin and enmity with God will not continue when a person is born again (1 John 3:9–10).

- The "gift of God," eternal life (Romans 6:23), includes all that pertains to life and godliness (2 Peter 1:3; Romans 8:32), not just a ticket to heaven.

- Jesus is Lord of all, and the faith He demands involves unconditional surrender (Romans 6:17–18; 10:9–10). He does not bestow eternal life on those whose hearts remain set against Him (James 4:6).

- Those who truly believe will love Christ (1 Peter 1:8–9; Romans 8:28–30; 1 Corinthians 16:22). They will therefore long to obey Him (John 14:15, 23).

- Behavior is an important test of faith. Obedience is evidence that one's faith is real (1 John 2:3). On the other hand, the person who remains unwilling to obey Christ does not evidence true faith (1 John 2:4).

- Genuine believers may stumble and fall, but they *will* persevere in the faith (1 Corinthians 1:8). Those who later turn completely away from the Lord show that they were never truly born again (1 John 2:19).

NOTES

Chapter 1: Lord of the Universe

1. Arthur W. Pink, *The Sovereignty of God* (Grand Rapids: Baker, 1930), 29–31, 245–52, 311–14.
2. Ibid., 29–30.
3. Ibid., 246.
4. Ibid., 314. The sections I quote here were removed in the edition of Pink's work published by The Banner of Truth Trust (1961). In his biography of Arthur Pink, editor Iain Murray called Pink's denial of God's love for the non-elect an "area of serious weakness." Iain Murray, *The Life of Arthur W. Pink* (Edinburgh: Banner of Truth, 1981), 196.

Chapter 3: Daily Submission

1. R. F. Delderfield, *The March of the Twenty-Six* (London: Hodder and Stoughton, 1962), 197.

Chapter 4: Holy Living

1. Charles Ryrie, *So Great Salvation* (Wheaton, IL: Victor, 1989), 49.
2. Benjamin B. Warfield, *Perfectionism* (Philadelphia: Presbyterian & Reformed, 1958), 356.

Chapter 5: Confession and Restoration

1. Louis Berkhof, *Systematic Theology* (Grand Rapids: Eerdmans, 1939), 486.

Chapter 6: Ultimate Destination

1. Obviously, a similar problem exists in Wesleyan and Arminian theology, and any other system of belief that makes room for Christians to fall away and lose their salvation.
2. John Calvin, *Institutes of the Christian Religion*, trans. Henry Beveridge, 3:2:7 (reprint, Grand Rapids: Eerdmans, 1966) 1:475.
3. Ibid., 1:484.
4. Zane Hodges sees great significance in this divergence between Calvin and those who came after him. Hodges even tries to enlist Calvin in support of the no-lordship position! (Zane Hodges, *Absolutely Free!* [Grand Rapids: Zondervan, 1989], 207–9, 214–15). Hodges, however, goes miles beyond Calvin on this issue, making assurance the sum and substance of

saving faith (pp. 50–51) and denying any need
for self-examination in the matter of assurance
(pp. 174–75). According to Hodges, assurance
is faith and vice versa. No other evidence of
regeneration is necessary. He assumes the great
Reformer taught the same thing. But whatever
Calvin's views on faith and assurance, it is
clear that he would have been no supporter
of Hodges's brand of no-lordship soteriology.
Calvin wrote, "We must take care not to separate
what the Lord perpetually conjoins. What then?
Let men be taught that it is impossible they can
be regarded as righteous by the merit of Christ,
without being renewed by his Spirit unto a holy
life. . . . *God receives none into favour who are not
also made truly righteous*." Henry Beveridge and
Jules Bonnet, eds., *Selected Works of John Calvin*,
7 vols. (reprint, Grand Rapids: Baker, 1983), 3:246
(emphasis added). Calvin added, "[Faith] is not a
bare knowledge which flutters in the mind, [but]
it carries along with it a lively affection, which
has its seat in the heart." Ibid., 250.

5. John Owen's writings on assurance are a
refreshing exception to this rule. Cf. Sinclair
B. Ferguson, *John Owens on the Christian Life*
(Edinburgh: Banner of Truth, 1987), 99–124.

6. "Faith totters if it pays attention to works,
since no one, even the most holy, will find

there anything on which to rely." John Calvin,
Institutes of the Christian Religion, trans. Ford
Lewis Battles (Philadelphia: Westminster, 1960),
3:11:11.

7. Bob Wilkin, "Putting the Gospel Debate in
Sharper Focus," *The Grace Evangelical Society
News* (May 1991): 1.

8. Assurance apart from sanctification is the
essence of antinomianism. And antinomianism
is often the result of an extreme emphasis on
assurance as the essence of faith. Even in the
early 1800s Charles Hodge noted that tendency:
"Those who make assurance the essence of faith,
generally reduce faith to a mere intellectual
assent. They are often censorious, refusing to
recognize as brethren those who do not agree
with them; and sometimes they are antinomian."
Charles Hodge, *Systematic Theology* (reprint,
Grand Rapids: Eerdmans, 1989), 3:106–7. Berkhof,
while recognizing the danger of antinomianism,
nevertheless saw that one can hold the position
that assurance is the essence of faith yet keep that
view in balance. He wrote, "Over against Rome
the position must be maintained that this sure
knowledge belongs to the essence of faith; and
in opposition to [antinomian] theologians such
as Sandeman, Wardlaw, Alexander, Chalmers,
and others, that a mere intellectual acceptance of

truth is not the whole of faith." Louis Berkhof,
Systematic Theology (Grand Rapids: Eerdmans,
1939), 503.

9. "In its NT context, the word [*assurance*] has
both objective and subjective references. As
objective, it denotes the ground of the believer's
confidence and certainty. . . . As subjective,
assurance has reference to the experience of
the believer. . . . Inward assurance must be
checked by moral and spiritual tests (cf. e.g.,
1 Cor. 6:9; Eph. 4:17; 1 John 2:3–5, etc.) by
which we know we are of the truth and that
our hearts are assured before God (1 John
3:19)." H. D. McDonald, "Assurance," *The
New International Dictionary of the Christian
Church* (Grand Rapids: Zondervan, 1978), 79.

10. Calvin, *Institutes of the Christian Religion*,
3:14:20, 2:87.

11. Ibid., 88.

12. "The grounds of assurance are more objective
than subjective; they are not so much within
us as without us. Hence the basis of assurance
must rest on sufficient objective evidence."
Robert F. Boyd, "Assurance," *Baker's Dictionary
of Theology* (Grand Rapids: Baker, 1960), 70.

13. John Owen, *The Works of John Owen*, 16 vols.
(reprint, London: Banner of Truth, 196), 6:549.

14. Ryrie, *So Great Salvation*, 141.

15. John Owen, *The Works of John Owen*, 6:605.

16. The test John is suggesting here is virtually identical to the self-examination Paul was calling for in 2 Corinthians 13:5: Does Jesus Christ live in you?

17. Zane Hodges, *Absolutely Free!* (Grand Rapids: Zondervan, 1989), 50–51.

18. Ibid., 31.

19. Owen, *The Works of John Owen*, 6:397.

20. Ibid., 6:396.

21. Ibid., 6:398.

22. Ibid., 6:397.

23. For a fuller discussion about assurance, see John MacArthur, *Saved Without a Doubt* (Wheaton, IL: Victor, 1992).

About the Author

Widely known for his thorough, candid approach to teaching God's Word, John MacArthur is a popular author and conference speaker and has served as pastor-teacher of Grace Community Church in Sun Valley, California, since 1969. John and his wife, Patricia, have four grown children and fifteen grandchildren.

John's pulpit ministry has been extended around the globe through his media ministry, Grace to You, and its satellite offices in seven countries. In addition to producing daily radio programs for nearly 2,000 English and Spanish radio outlets worldwide, Grace to You distributes books, software, audiotapes, and CDs by John MacArthur.

John is president of The Master's College and Seminary and has written hundreds of books and study guides, each one biblical and practical. Bestselling titles include *The Gospel According to Jesus*, *The Truth War*, *The Murder of Jesus*, *Twelve Ordinary Men*,

Twelve Extraordinary Women, and *The MacArthur Study Bible,* a 1998 ECPA Gold Medallion recipient.

For more details about John MacArthur and his Bible-teaching resources, contact Grace to You at 800-55-GRACE or www.gty.org.

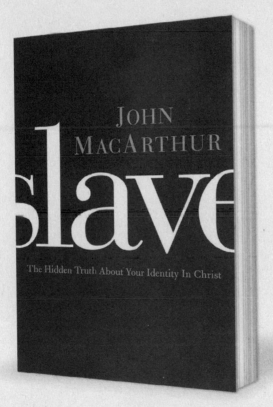